A First Atlas

Text: Sue Hook, Angela Royston
Consultant: Keith Lye B.A. Hons. (Bristol); F.R.G.S.
Maps: Contour Publishing
Computer illustrations: Mel Pickering
Watercolor iIllustrations: Lindy Norton
Photo Research: Liz Eddison
Editorial Director: Sue Hook
Art Director: Belinda Webster
Production Director: Lorraine Estelle
Assistant Editors: Samantha Hilton, Deborah Kespert
Co-editions Editors: Mathew Birch, Robert Sved

U.S. Editorial Team
Editorial Director: Carolyn Jackson
Cover Design: Karen Hudson
Assistant Editor: Mimi George
Text Contributor: Karen Burns Kellaher
Grateful acknowledgment is made to Adele Brodkin and Theron Cole.

Photo credits: Robert Aberman/The Hutchinson Library: p55; Brian and Cherry Alexander: p16, p17 (top); Tom Ang/Robert Harding: p41 (top); Gary Bell/Planet Earth Pictures: p83; R I M Campbell/Bruce Coleman: p44; John Cancalosi/Bruce Coleman: p84 (bottom); Alain Compost/Bruce Coleman: p79 (top); G&P Corrigan/Robert Harding: p68 (top); Rob Cousins/Robert Harding: p34 (bottom); Tim Defrisco/Allsport: p19 (bottom); Bernd Ducke/Britstock-IFA: p61; John Egan/The Hutchinson Library: p72; Everts/Britstock-IFA: p50; Financial Times/Robert Harding: p66; JG Fuller/The Hutchinson Library: p30; Francisco Futil/Bruce Coleman: p67 (top); Ron Gilling/Panos Pictures: p46, p78; Laurent Giradou/Robert Harding: p33 (bottom); Grafenhain/Britstock-IFA: p51 (top), p54; Z Harasym/Trip: p57; Jeremy Hartley/Panos Pictures: p40; D&J Heaton/Spectrum Colour Library: p79 (bottom); Jay/Britstock-IFA: p62; M Jenkin/Trip: p60; A A Johnson/Spectrum Colour Library: p43; Alexander Kuznetsov/Trip: p63 (bottom); David Lomax/Robert Harding: p67 (bottom); L C Marigo/Bruce Coleman: p32 (left); New Zealand Consulate: p84 (top); Mark Newman/FLPA: p63 (top); S Pern/The Hutchinson Library: p36; Pictor International: p37, p74 (top), p74 (bottom); Picturepoint: p34 (top), p73 (top); Pictures Colour Library: p19 (top), p41 (bottom), p47 (top), p53; Dr Eckart Pott/Bruce Coleman: p51 (bottom); Hans Reinhard/Bruce Coleman: p82 (top); Geoff Renner/Robert Harding: p24; Sean Sprague/Panos Pictures: p35; Tony Stone Associates: p18, p22 (top), p27 (top), p27 (bottom), p33 (top), p52 (top), p52 (bottom), p68 (bottom); Telegraph Colour Library: p26, p42, p73 (bottom); Trip: p75 (bottom); Penny Tweedie/Panos Pictures: p82 (bottom); Philip Wolmuth/Panos Pictures: p31 (top); Adam Woolfitt/Robert Harding: p25 (top), p85; ZEFA: p17 (bottom), p22 (bottom), p23 (top), p23 (bottom), p25 (bottom), p31 (bottom), p32 (right), p45, p47 (bottom), p69, p75 (top), p87.

Produced for Scholastic Inc. by Two-Can Publishing Ltd., 346 Old Street, London, EC1V 9NQ, U.K.
ISBN: 0-590-47528-2
12 11 10 9 8 7 6 5 4 3 2 1   6 7 8 9/9 0 1/0

Printed in the U.S.A.   09
Color reproduction by Daylight Colour Art Pte Ltd., Singapore.
First Scholastic printing, January 1996.

A First Atlas

Scholastic
Reference

SCHOLASTIC INC.

New York Toronto London Auckland Sydney

How to use this book

Look it up!
An atlas is designed to help you look for information about the many places in the world. This one is organized by geographical regions. You can find them listed on the Contents page.

Pronunciation
Some words, such as encyclopedia (en-SY-clo-PEE-dee-a), are difficult to say. To say them correctly, make the sounds in the parentheses after each of the words. The sounds spelled with all capital letters are pronounced with more stress, or emphasis.

Cross-references
Above the colored bar on each map there is a list of entries in the other three books in the *Scholastic First Encyclopedia*, with their book titles. These entries tell you more about the subject on the page.

Contents
The Contents page at the front of the book lists the main entries, or subjects in the book, and which page they are on.

Glossary
Words in the book that may be difficult to understand are marked in **bold**. The Glossary near the back of the book lists these words and explains what they mean.

Index
The Index at the back of the book is a list of everything mentioned in the book, arranged in alphabetical order, with its page number. If an entry is in *italics*, it means that it is a label on a map. If only the page number is in *italics*, the entry appears in the main text as well as being a map label.

Contents

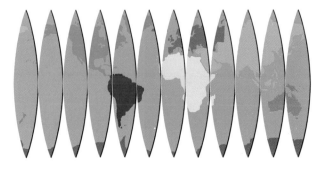

The earth

The earth is a huge ball floating in space. Scientists believe that more than four and one-half billion years ago it was a tiny speck of dust in a cloud of gas that formed our sun and solar system. The earth became at first a ball of super-hot liquid material. During millions of years a thin layer of lava and rock cooled and hardened. This became the earth's crust. The crust has cracks, called faults, in it. Sudden movements of the crust cause **volcanic eruptions** and **earthquakes** near the faults.

Drifting continents

The world's continents rest on huge pieces of the earth's crust, called plates.

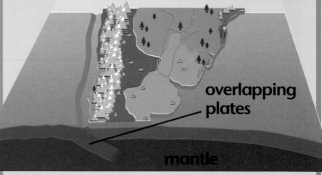

continent of South America

overlapping plates

mantle

The plates float like rafts on the super-hot, liquid mantle beneath.

Inside the earth

The earth is made of layers of rock, like layers of skin on an onion.

At the center is the inner core, made of very hot iron and as big as our moon.

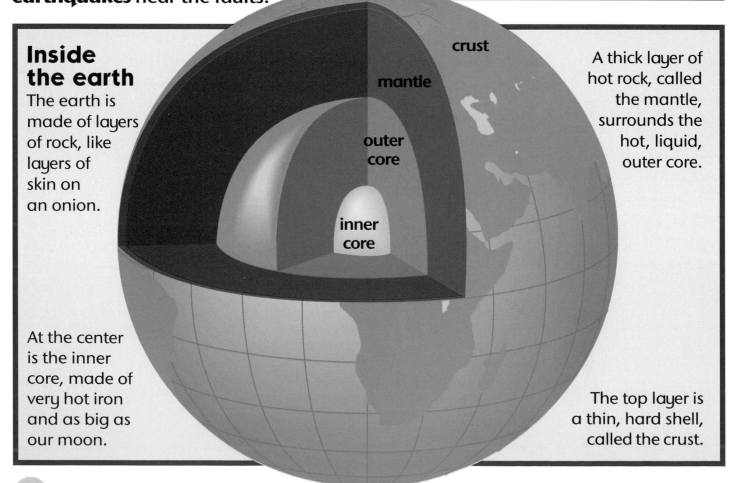

crust

mantle

outer core

inner core

A thick layer of hot rock, called the mantle, surrounds the hot, liquid, outer core.

The top layer is a thin, hard shell, called the crust.

Ancient earth

Scientists believe that the seven continents that make up our world today were once joined together. They formed a huge jigsaw of land, which was the super-continent Pangaca (Pan-JAY-uh).

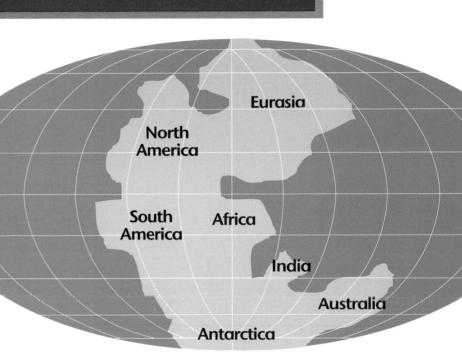

▲ The earth (Pangaea) 200 million years ago

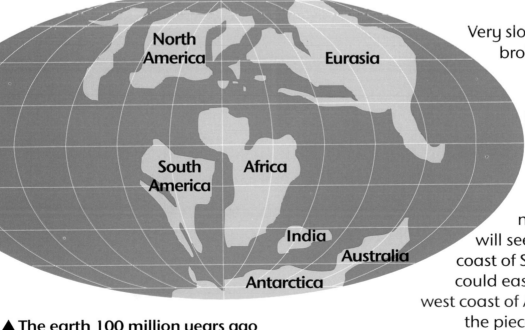

▲ The earth 100 million years ago

Very slowly, Pangaea broke into pieces, which moved apart. Each piece became a continent. Look at the map of the world on the next page. You will see that the east coast of South America could easily fit onto the west coast of Africa, just like the pieces in a puzzle.

Maps and mapmakers

A First Atlas is a book of maps of our world. Maps are flat pictures of the earth. The maps in this book show you the shapes of the earth's land, oceans, and seas, and where they are. Maps also show you where the hot and cold places are in the world.

Making maps

The earth is round, like a ball, but maps are flat. Try peeling an orange, keeping the skin in one piece. Now try to lay the skin flat on a table. You have to squash some pieces and stretch others. This is what mapmakers must do to draw maps of the earth.

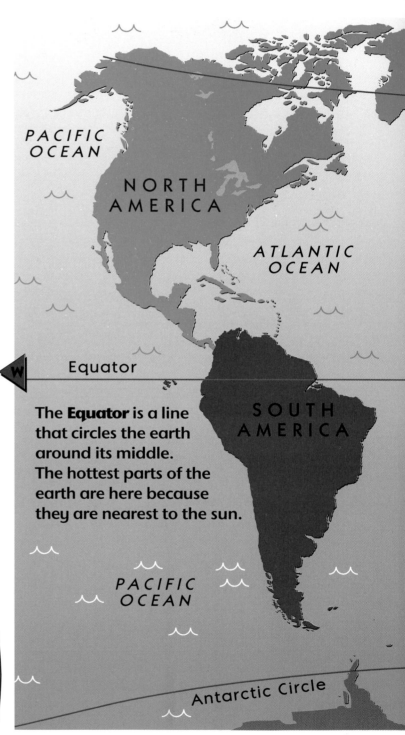

PACIFIC OCEAN

NORTH AMERICA

ATLANTIC OCEAN

Equator

The **Equator** is a line that circles the earth around its middle. The hottest parts of the earth are here because they are nearest to the sun.

SOUTH AMERICA

PACIFIC OCEAN

Antarctic Circle

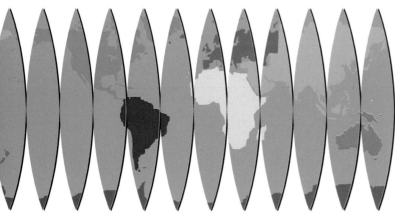

▲ This is how the earth would look if it were laid out flat. There are big gaps at the top and bottom.

Four big oceans and many seas cover more than half of the earth. You can find the names of the oceans on the map of the world.

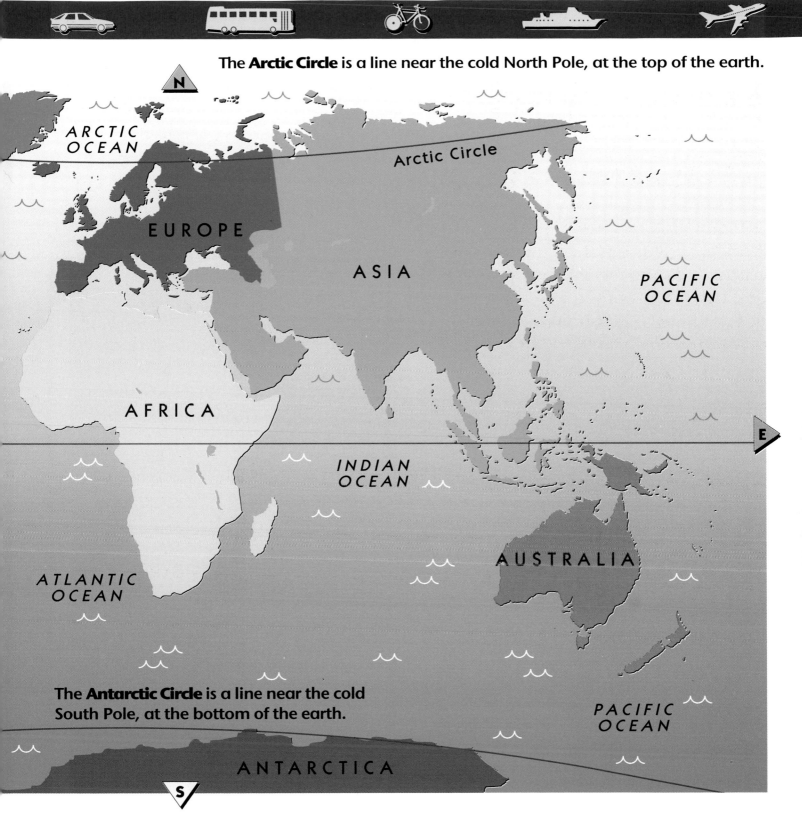

The **Arctic Circle** is a line near the cold North Pole, at the top of the earth.

N

ARCTIC OCEAN

Arctic Circle

EUROPE

ASIA

PACIFIC OCEAN

AFRICA

E

INDIAN OCEAN

ATLANTIC OCEAN

AUSTRALIA

The **Antarctic Circle** is a line near the cold South Pole, at the bottom of the earth.

PACIFIC OCEAN

ANTARCTICA

S

Land that is not covered by water is divided into huge areas called continents. You can see the seven continents on the map.

The earth's continents are divided into countries. Today, there are 191 countries. Each has its own people, flag, and customs.

11

Looking at maps

To show us places and landforms on maps, mapmakers use picture **symbols**, signs, labels, and lines in different colors.

They are like a code that we need to understand in order to read the maps.

Labels
Labels tell you names of places on maps. Here are the kinds of things labelled in this atlas.

ocean	*INDIAN OCEAN*
sea	Arabian Sea
island	*Sumatra*
country	**JAPAN**
desert	Sahara Desert
forest	*Amazon Rainforest*
mountain	**Rocky Mountains**
river	Mississippi River
lake	Lake Michigan
capital city	☆ **Washington, D.C.**
city	**Los Angeles**

The meaning of lines
Mapmakers draw some lines to show where countries and continents begin and end. These lines are called borders. They do not exist on the land; they only exist on the maps.

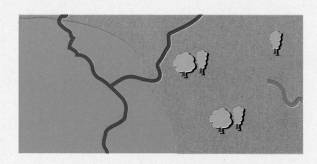

Red lines show the borders between countries.

Purple lines show the borders between continents.

Land signs
Picture symbols show you different kinds of land on maps.

grassland
There are grass-covered lands all over the world. Sometimes they are called savannah or pampas. Grassland is the best land for farming.

desert
Desert areas have almost no rain. Most deserts are hot and dry in the day, but cold at night. Fewer animals and plants survive here than in most other landforms.

deciduous
Deciduous trees, such as beech, birch, and oak, lose their leaves in the fall. Deciduous forests grow in cool areas.

tundra
Tundra is cold, bare **plain** near the Arctic Circle. The surface of the ground is frozen all year so the growing season is very short.

ice and snow
Thick ice covers the areas around the North and South Poles, and big storms bring snow and strong winds.

rainforest
Most rainforests grow in tropical areas near the **Equator**, where it is hot and wet. Rainforests are home to millions of different plants and animals.

evergreen forest
Evergreen trees such as pine, fir, spruce, and larch stay green all year round. Evergreen forests grow mostly in cold areas.

mountains
Many areas of the world are covered in high, rocky mountains. Very high mountains are covered in snow.

Where are you going next?
On each map, the little red airplane points the way to the next **region** you will find in the book.

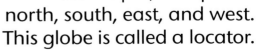

Where are you?
On each map, a small **globe** shows where in the world the map is, and points north, south, east, and west. This globe is called a locator.

Canada and the Arctic

Canada is the second largest country in the world. Only Russia is bigger. This huge country lies at the top of the North American continent. To its north is the icy Arctic Ocean, which surrounds the North Pole. To its south is the United States. Canada has 12 **provinces and territories.** Those in the north are cold and rugged, so few people live there. Most big cities are in the warmer south.

Did you know?

Canada's lakes hold a third of the world's fresh water.

There is no land at the North Pole. It is made up of ice up to 30 feet thick.

On the border between Canada and the U.S. are the Niagara Falls. One year, 150 years ago, it was so cold that these great waterfalls froze over.

NORWAY

Arctic Circle

RUSSIA

Greenland (DENMARK)

Ellesmere Island

Queen Elizabeth Islands

North Pole

A R C T I C   O C E A N

Banks Island

RUSSIA

Bering Straits

Alaska (U.S.A.)

ICELAND

NORTH ATLANTIC OCEAN

Newfoundland

Prince Edward Island

New Brunswick

Nova Scotia

CANADA

Quebec

Montreal

St. Lawrence River

Ottawa

Niagara Falls

Lake Ontario

Lake Erie

Toronto

Lake Huron

Lake Michigan

Ontario

Lake Superior

Great Lakes

Baffin Island

Hudson Bay

Northwest Territories

Victoria Island

Nelson River

Lake Winnipeg

Manitoba

Churchill River

Great Bear Lake

Great Slave Lake

Lake Athabasca

Saskatchewan

Alberta

Mackenzie River

Calgary

UNITED STATES OF AMERICA

Yukon Territory

Rocky Mountains

British Columbia

Vancouver

Vancouver Island

Land on this map

mountains

grassland

deciduous forest

evergreen forest

tundra

ice and snow

S

Northern Canada and the Arctic

The Arctic is the area around the North Pole. It includes the north of Canada. It is farther north than any other place on earth. In the long, dark winter, most of the Arctic is so cold that the land and the ocean stay frozen. No trees or plants grow. In the short summer, some of the ice melts. Then, tiny plants and flowers bloom. Despite the cold, the Inuit (IN-oo-it) people have lived in the Arctic for thousands of years.

▲ During an arctic winter the Inuit must dig through thick ice to find fresh water.

Animals and plants

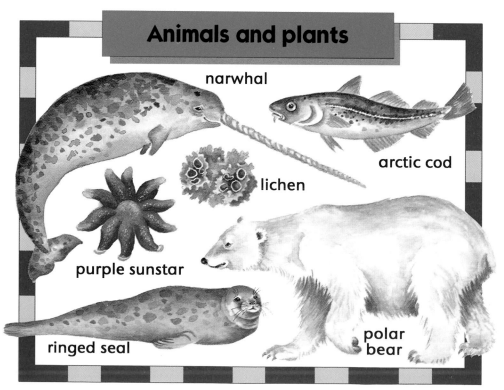

narwhal

arctic cod

lichen

purple sunstar

ringed seal

polar bear

The Inuit live in towns built on top of the ice. Some fish or hunt for bears and **caribou**. Others work in gold, tin, and copper mines. They travel by snowmobile or sled. The Inuit are used to cold weather. They even have 20 different words for 20 different kinds of snow!

There are thousands of icebergs in the Arctic and North Atlantic oceans. Some of these huge floating chunks of ice are as big as mountains. Only the tip of the iceberg shows above the water.

now picture this

An arctic iceberg once floated 2,500 miles south to the island of Bermuda, where the water is much warmer, without melting.

▲ The Inuit build igloos from slabs of ice. They sleep in them during long hunting trips.

◄ Skidoos or snowmobiles carry equipment and supplies across the arctic ice deserts.

Southern Canada

Southern Canada is a mix of cities, lakes, forests, **plains**, and mountains. Many Canadians live in the east, near the Great Lakes and St. Lawrence River. This area is home to factories, farms, and miles of evergreen forest. In the middle of Southern Canada are flat plains where farmers raise cattle and grow fields of wheat. In the west, people can hike or ski in the Rocky Mountains.

The Inuit (IN-oo-it), Cree, and other native peoples were the first Canadians. Even today, some cities' names, such as Ottawa, come from native words. Then, the French and English settled in Canada. Today, nearly all Canadians speak English, French, or both.

Most Canadians live in southern cities. In the southeast are Montreal and Toronto, the country's two largest cities. Here, cars and other products are made. The south-western city of Calgary is the oil center of Canada. Vancouver is an important **port** on the Pacific Ocean.

▶ Calgary is one of the fastest growing cities in Canada.

Animals and plants

beaver

grizzly bear

maple

pine

moose

raccoon

Natural resources help make Canada a wealthy nation. One of Canada's biggest industries is timber, or wood. The country has more pine and spruce trees than any other place in the world. Companies use wood from the trees to make paper and lumber.

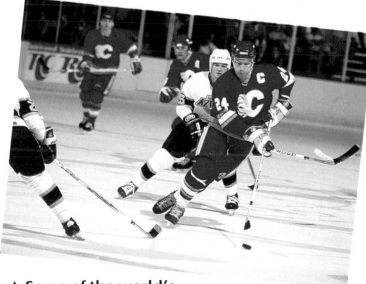

▲ Some of the world's best ice hockey players are Canadian.

The United States and Mexico

The United States of America is the world's fourth largest country. Within its borders are thick forests, wide **plains**, deep **canyons**, snow-capped mountains, huge lakes, hot deserts, and modern cities. Native Americans have lived here for thousands of years. Then, 500 years ago, other people began coming from all over the world.

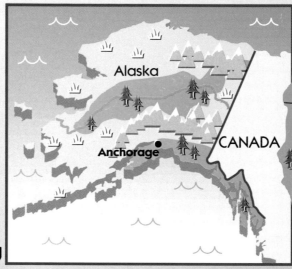

Did you know?

Mexico City, Mexico, is one of the world's most crowded cities. It has twenty million people. If they all joined hands, they would reach halfway around the world.

The Grand Canyon in Arizona is more than 5,000 feet deep in some spots. That's almost one mile. Mules bring mail to the few people who choose to live there.

The United States is divided into 50 **states**. Two, Alaska and Hawaii, are not connected by land to the others. Alaska is next to Canada in the northwest. Hawaii is a group of **volcanic islands** in the Pacific Ocean. These states have been moved onto this map to show all the states together.

The country of Mexico is south of the United States. The two countries are separated by the Rio Grande, which means Big River. Mountains run along the east and west coasts. The rest of the country is mostly dry desert. Most Mexicans live in the middle of the country near the capital, Mexico City.

Hawaii

PACIFIC OCEAN

CANADA

Montana

North Dakota

Minnesota

Lake Superior

Mount Washington

Maine

South Dakota

Wisconsin

Lake Huron

Lake Ontario

Vermont

New Hampshire

Wyoming

Mount Rushmore

Lake Michigan

Michigan

Niagara Falls

New York

Boston

STATES OF AMERICA

Detroit

Lake Erie

Connecticut

Massachusetts

Rocky Mountains

Chicago

Pennsylvania

Rhode Island

Nebraska

Iowa

Indiana

Ohio

Philadelphia

New York City

New Jersey

Colorado River

Missouri River

Illinois

Washington, D.C.

Delaware

Colorado

Kansas

Missouri

West Virginia

Maryland

ATLANTIC OCEAN

Great Plains

Ohio River

Kentucky

Appalachian Mountains

Virginia

New Mexico

Oklahoma

Arkansas

Tennessee

North Carolina

N

Mississippi River

South Carolina

W

E

Dallas

Mississippi

Atlanta

Georgia

Texas

Louisiana

Alabama

Houston

New Orleans

Florida

Rio Grande

Kennedy Space Center

S

MEXICO

Gulf of Mexico

Miami

Mexico City

Mount Popocatépetl

Acapulco

BELIZE

Land on this map

	desert		evergreen forest
	mountains		rainforest
	grassland		tundra
	deciduous forest		

GUATEMALA

The Northeast

The Northeast **region** of the United States stretches from Maine to Pennsylvania. This region is the most crowded part of the country. Millions of people live in the big cities of Boston, New York, and Philadelphia along the coast of the Atlantic Ocean. The Northeast has tall forests, beautiful beaches, and rolling hills.

The Northeast is where Europeans first settled hundreds of years ago. Many English people came here. Part of the Northeast region is still called New England.

▲ Winter in the Northeast can be very cold. These kids live in Vermont, close to the U.S. border with Canada.

▲ Old European-style buildings are found in the Northeast.

People in the Northeast have many kinds of jobs. Most people work in business or have jobs that serve the public, like teaching or nursing.

Farmers grow apples and other crops and raise cows for milk. In New England, they make syrup from maple tree sugar. Some people who live near the coast fish for tuna and codfish.

▼ The world's first skyscrapers were built on Manhattan Island in New York City.

The Appalachian Trail is the longest marked hiking path in the world. It runs through the Appalachian Mountains. The trail stretches 2,000 miles from Maine to Georgia. It passes through 14 states. It takes about four months to walk the whole trail.

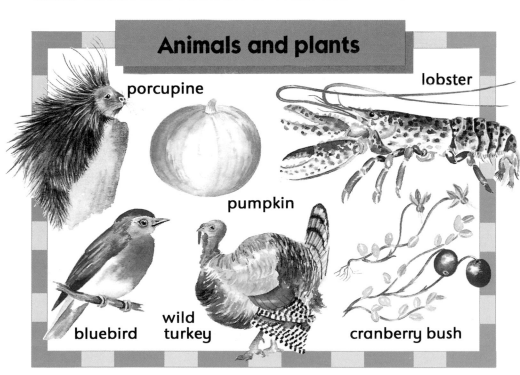

Animals and plants

porcupine

lobster

pumpkin

bluebird

wild turkey

cranberry bush

▲ New York City's Statue of Liberty stands for freedom.

23

The Midwest and West

The Midwest is a large **region** in the middle of the United States. It stretches from the Great Lakes in the Northeast to the Rocky Mountains in the West. The Midwest includes Chicago, Detroit, and other big cities near the Great Lakes. It also has flat farmland called the Great Plains. On the other side of the Rocky Mountains are the western **states**. These states have tall forests, **fertile valleys,** and beaches by the Pacific Ocean.

▼ The heads of Presidents George Washington, Thomas Jefferson, Theodore Roosevelt, and Abraham Lincoln are carved out of Mount Rushmore, in South Dakota.

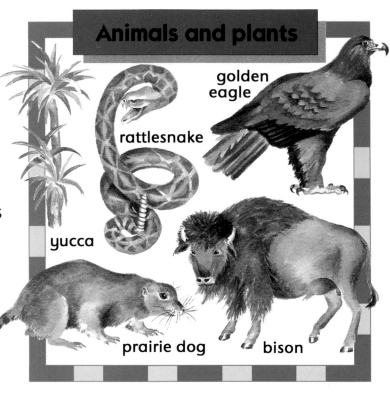

Animals and plants

golden eagle

rattlesnake

yucca

prairie dog

bison

The Midwest is known as the Farm Belt. On its flat **plains**, or prairies, farmers grow half of the country's corn and much of its wheat and soy beans.

Boats called barges carry grain and other goods from the Midwest down the Mississippi River to **ports** on the Gulf of Mexico. There the goods are put onto bigger ships and sent to other countries.

The Great Divide runs north to south through the Rocky Mountains. On one side of the divide, rivers flow east and on the other, they flow west.

Many people visit the Rocky Mountain states of Colorado and Wyoming to ski and look at the spectacular scenery.

▼ Monument Valley in Utah has red **sandstone** formations that are 1,000 feet tall. A building this high would have 80 stories.

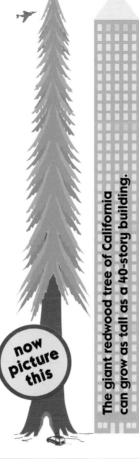

now picture this

The giant redwood tree of California can grow as tall as a 40-story building.

▲ In New Mexico, people mine silver and use it to make beautiful jewelry.

California is the third largest state, with big cities like Los Angeles and San Francisco. Many people live in California because of its wonderful **climate** and natural beauty. There are beaches and old redwood forests. Wine-making and computers are big industries there. In Hollywood, thousands of movies are made each year.

The South

The warm southern states run from Texas on the Gulf of Mexico, to Virginia on the coast of the Atlantic Ocean. The southern states have rich farmland. They grow much of the country's fruit, vegetables, and cotton. Cattle ranches and oil fields dot Texas, the country's second largest **state**.

Animals and plants

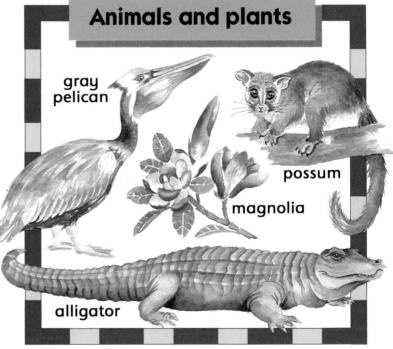

gray pelican

possum

magnolia

alligator

▲ Kennedy Space Center is at Cape Canaveral in Florida. The first person to land on the moon was launched in a rocket from here.

Florida is farther south than any other state. Because its **climate** is warm and sunny, millions of people vacation there. They visit Disneyworld and go to beaches. Many Americans move to Florida when they retire. Miami is a center of international business and banking as well as a resort.

Mexico

Mexico is a mountainous country south of the United States. Much of Mexico's land is too dry or rugged for farming. In places where the land is good, farmers grow much of the world's corn, coffee, and cotton. Other Mexicans live in cities where there are large factories. Mexico also has silver mines and factories. Many tourists visit Mexico to enjoy its historical places and beautiful beaches.

► Mexican craftworkers make and sell pottery, baskets, and silver jewelry. They follow beautiful, old designs.

▼ These ruins of an ancient city are found on Mexico's Yucatan (YOU-cah-tan) **peninsula.**

About 500 years ago, Native Americans called Aztecs built cities with canals and large buildings. Then people from Spain took over Mexico. Today, most Mexicans have Native American and Spanish **ancestors.**

Mexico's cities are very crowded. The country has 115 people in every square mile. That is more than ninety million people.

27

Central and South America

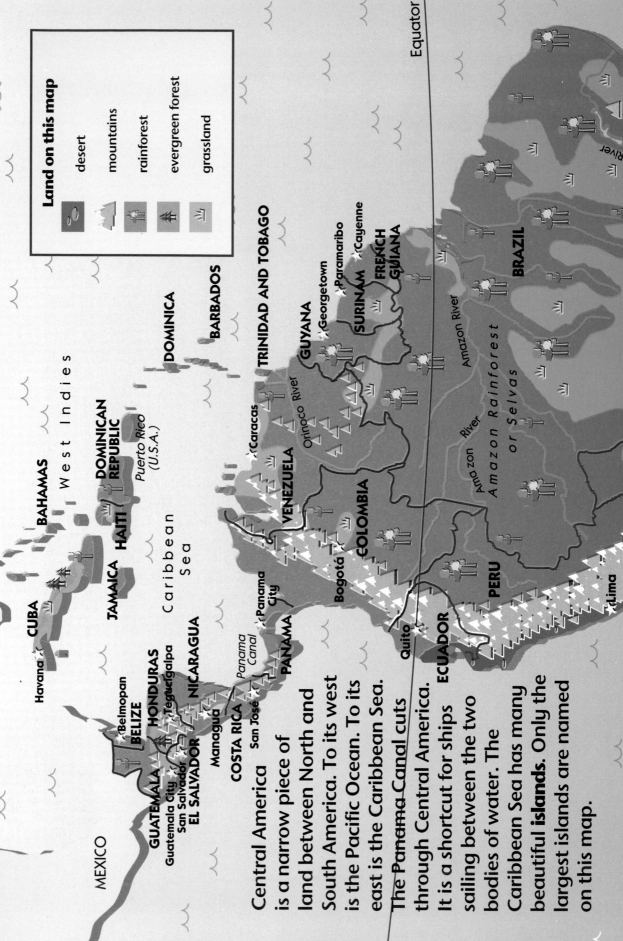

Land on this map

- desert
- mountains
- rainforest
- evergreen forest
- grassland

MEXICO

BAHAMAS
West Indies

CUBA
Havana

BELIZE
Belmopan
GUATEMALA
Guatemala City
San Salvador
EL SALVADOR
HONDURAS
Tegucigalpa
NICARAGUA
Managua
COSTA RICA
San José
PANAMA
Panama City
Panama Canal

JAMAICA

HAITI
DOMINICAN REPUBLIC
Puerto Rico (U.S.A.)

Caribbean Sea

DOMINICA

BARBADOS

TRINIDAD AND TOBAGO

VENEZUELA
Caracas
Orinoco River

COLOMBIA
Bogotá

GUYANA
Georgetown
SURINAM
Paramaribo
FRENCH GUIANA
Cayenne

ECUADOR
Quito

PERU
Lima

Amazon River
Amazon River
Amazon Rainforest or Selvas

BRAZIL

River

Equator

Central America is a narrow piece of land between North and South America. To its west is the Pacific Ocean. To its east is the Caribbean Sea. The Panama Canal cuts through Central America. It is a shortcut for ships sailing between the two bodies of water. The Caribbean Sea has many beautiful islands. Only the largest islands are named on this map.

PACIFIC OCEAN

ATLANTIC OCEAN

N
W
E
S

São Francisco

Rio de Janeiro

São Paulo

Brasília ★

Paraguay River

Gran Chaco

Asunción ★

PARAGUAY

BOLIVIA

URUGUAY

Montevideo ★

Uruguay River

Paraná River

Buenos Aires ★

pampas

ARGENTINA

Falkland Islands (U.K.)

Machu Picchu

Cuzco

Lake Titicaca

La Paz ★

Atacama Desert

Andes Mountains

Patagonia

Santiago ★

CHILE

Tierra del Fuego

Ushuaia

Cape Horn

Did you know?

Howler monkeys in the rainforests of Central America are the world's noisiest animals. Their calls can be heard from 10 miles away.

There are about twelve thousand islands in the Caribbean Sea, but people live on only 185 of them.

South America's tropical rainforest, the Selvas, is the largest in the world.

The continent of South America is shaped like a long triangle. Most of it is south of the **Equator.** That makes it summer here when it is winter in North America. The **climate** changes greatly as you travel south. The north and middle of the continent are hot and rainy. The southern tip is cold and barren, close to the icy continent of Antarctica.

Central America

The seven countries of Panama, Guatemala, Belize, Costa Rica, El Salvador, Honduras, and Nicaragua form mainland Central America. The **climate** here is mostly hot and rainy. Some countries have thick rainforests filled with thousands of kinds of plants and animals. Central America also has many **volcanoes**. Some of them are active.

▲ These Mayan women are preparing yarn to sell at a Guatemalan market.

Animals and plants

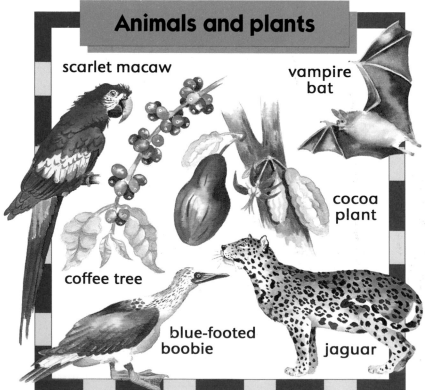

scarlet macaw

vampire bat

cocoa plant

coffee tree

blue-footed boobie

jaguar

Today, most Central Americans speak Spanish. Their **ancestors** came from Spain or Africa, or they may have been in Central America thousands of years, like the Maya. Most people make their living by farming. Some have their own small farms. Others work on large cotton, sugar, coffee, or banana plantations. Some farming methods are bad for the rainforests, so people are looking for ways to protect them.

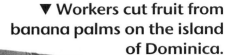

The West Indies

The **islands** in the Caribbean Sea have beautiful beaches and sunny weather. Many, like the Bahamas and Jamaica, are popular vacation spots. Some West Indian people work in the tourist industry. Others fish, grow fruit, or work on coffee or sugar plantations.

▼ Workers cut fruit from banana palms on the island of Dominica.

▼ This beautiful beach, made of white **coral** sand, is on the West Indian island of Tobago.

Tropical South America

Brazil, Venezuela, Surinam, French Guiana (Gee-AHN-ah), and Guyana make up tropical South America. These countries are hot and rainy. Much of the land is covered in thick rainforest. The mighty Amazon River runs through the rainforest to the Atlantic Ocean. Along the Atlantic coast are big modern cities, such as Rio de Janeiro in Brazil, and Caracas in Venezuela.

Although most people live in cities and towns, some native peoples still live deep in the Amazon rainforest. Each tribe, or group, has its own language and customs. The forest provides everything, from medicines to building materials. Some use the juice from rainforest plants to protect themselves from insect bites.

▶ On special occasions, the Kanelo people use paints from plants to cover their bodies.

▼ Yanomami hunters tip their arrows with deadly animal poisons.

▲ Rio de Janeiro, in Brazil, is the second largest city in South America after São Paulo.

Carnival time

Many South American cities have a huge party every fall. It is called Carnival. For four days and nights, people dress in colorful costumes.

▶ People dancing in one of the many Carnival parades in Brazil.

Animals and plants

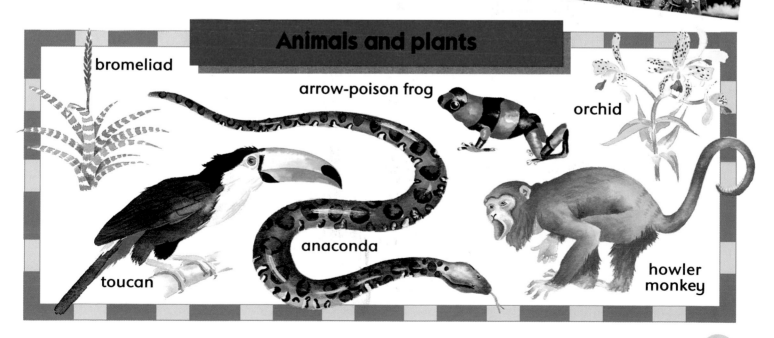

bromeliad

arrow-poison frog

orchid

toucan

anaconda

howler monkey

The Countries of the Andes

The Andes Mountains stretch through six countries — Colombia, Ecuador (ECK-wah-door), Peru, Bolivia, Chile (CHILL-ee), and Argentina. These mountains are longer than the United States is wide. Some of them are active **volcanoes**. About half of the people who live in this **region** are native Indians called Quechas (KETCH-ahs). Others are **descendants** of people who came from Spain 500 years ago.

▶ The ruins of Macchu Picchu are on an Andes mountaintop in Peru. This walled city was built by the ancient Inca people about 500 years ago.

La Paz, the capital of Bolivia, is very high in the Andes Mountains. Because it is so high, it is very cold. It is so cold that crops and trees cannot grow. Nearby is Lake Titicaca. On this lake are **islands** full of ancient Inca temples.

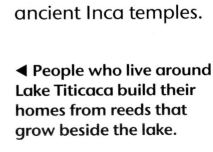

◀ People who live around Lake Titicaca build their homes from reeds that grow beside the lake.

In Peru, Bolivia, and Ecuador mountain farmers grow beans, gourds, potatoes, and corn. They keep llamas and alpacas for their wool and meat. Some workers mine gold, silver, and copper.

The Atacama Desert, in Chile, lies between the Pacific coast and the Andes Mountains. It is the driest desert in the world and has almost no plants or people. In 1971, part of this desert had its first rainfall in 400 years!

▼ Fresh fruit and vegetables are brought by truck to this Bolivian market from the warm, **fertile valleys** below the mountains.

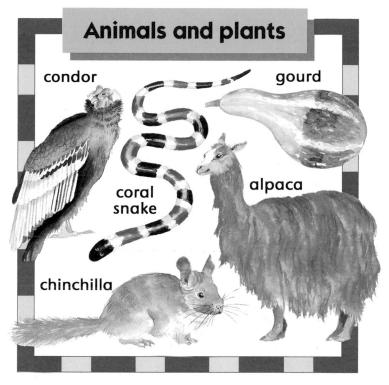

Animals and plants

condor

gourd

coral snake

alpaca

chinchilla

Southern South America

Paraguay (PAR-a-gwhy), Uruguay (YOUR-a-gwhy), southern Chile, and Argentina make up Southern South America. Much of the land is pampas. These are grassy **plains** good for raising sheep and cattle. Even though the southern tip of South America is stormy and freezing cold, it is called Tierra del Fuego, or Land of Fire. Spanish explorers gave it this name 500 years ago when they saw Indians there building campfires.

▼ In Argentina, cowboys called gauchos (GOW-chose) round up cattle on the pampas.

Most of Paraguay is a dry, windy plain called the Gran Chaco. Very few people live there. Most people live in the east. Uruguay, one of the smallest countries in South America, has sheep farms and a growing tourist industry.

Argentina is the largest country in Southern South America. One out of every three Argentinians lives in the capital city of Buenos Aires. On the pampas of central Argentina, there are cattle ranches. To the west of Argentina is Chile. Southern Chile is one of the world's wettest and stormiest places.

▼ Cold winds from Antarctica bring snow and ice to Patagonia.

now picture this

If you sailed east around the world from Ushuaia you would end up back where you started without ever seeing land.

N

W

E

S

Patagonia is a very cold, windy **region** in southern Argentina. There are no trees here, but there is lots of grass for sheep to eat. In the far south, there are snow-capped **volcanoes**, **geysers**, waterfalls, lakes, and **islands**. The town of Ushuaia (ooh-SHY-ah), near Cape Horn, is farther south than any other town in the world.

Animals and plants

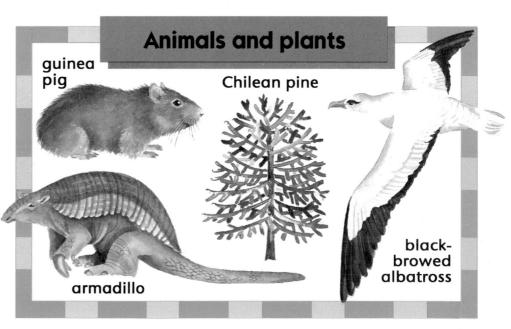

guinea pig

Chilean pine

armadillo

black-browed albatross

37

Africa

The continent of Africa has 53 countries, more than any other continent. Africa is cut in half by the **Equator**, a line drawn by mapmakers around the middle of the world. The sun's rays are strong near the Equator, so most of Africa is very hot. In North Africa is the dry, vast Sahara Desert. In the middle of the continent, near the Equator, the land is covered by rainforest. Much of East and Southern Africa is covered with rich grasslands.

Did you know?

The hottest place in the world is Al-Aziziyah, Libya, in the Sahara Desert. One day in 1922, it was over 136° **Fahrenheit** in the shade!

More than 1,000 different languages are spoken in Africa.

Some parts of Africa get up to 100 inches of rain a year. In other parts, rain may not fall for six or seven years.

Red Sea

Mediterranean Sea

Nile River

Cairo

EGYPT

ERITREA

Asmera

Khartoum

Tunis

TUNISIA

Tripoli

Al-Aziziyah

LIBYA

CHAD

Algiers

Atlas Mountains

ALGERIA

Sahara Desert

NIGER

Fez

Rabat

MOROCCO

El Aaiún

Niger River

MALI

MAURITANIA

Nouakchott

Canary Islands (SPAIN)

WESTERN SAHARA

Dakar

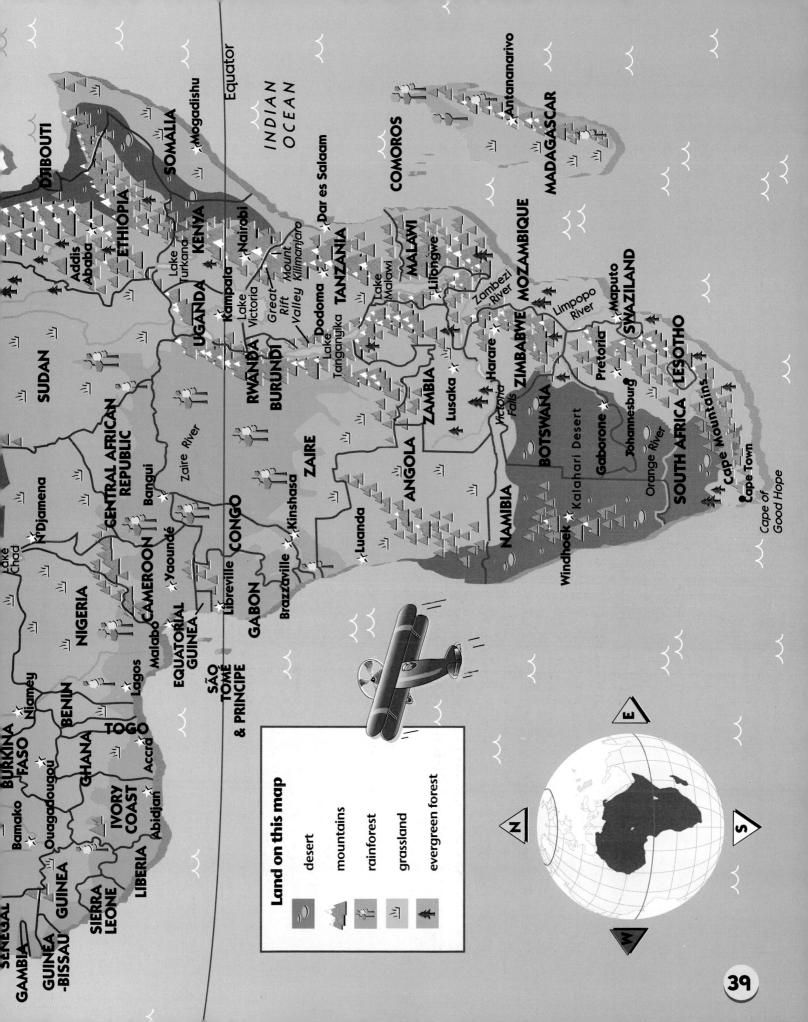

INDIAN OCEAN

Equator

DJIBOUTI

SOMALIA
Mogadishu

ETHIOPIA
Addis Ababa

KENYA
Nairobi

UGANDA
Kampala

Lake Turkana

Lake Victoria

Mount Kilimanjaro

Great Rift Valley

Dodoma

TANZANIA
Dar es Salaam

Lake Tanganyika

RWANDA
BURUNDI

SUDAN

CENTRAL AFRICAN REPUBLIC
Bangui

Zaire River

ZAIRE

Kinshasa

CONGO
Brazzaville

GABON
Libreville

CAMEROON
Yaoundé

EQUATORIAL GUINEA
Malabo

SÃO TOMÉ & PRINCIPE

NIGERIA
Lagos

BENIN

TOGO

GHANA
Accra

BURKINA FASO
Ouagadougou

Niamey

IVORY COAST
Abidjan

LIBERIA

SIERRA LEONE

GUINEA

GUINEA-BISSAU

GAMBIA

SENEGAL

Bamako

Lake Chad

N'Djamena

COMOROS

MADAGASCAR
Antananarivo

MALAWI
Lilongwe

Lake Malawi

MOZAMBIQUE

Zambezi River

ZAMBIA
Lusaka

ANGOLA
Luanda

Victoria Falls

ZIMBABWE
Harare

Limpopo River

BOTSWANA

Kalahari Desert

Gaborone

NAMIBIA
Windhoek

Orange River

Johannesburg

Pretoria

SWAZILAND
Maputo

LESOTHO

SOUTH AFRICA

Cape Mountains

Cape Town

Cape of Good Hope

Land on this map

desert	
mountains	
rainforest	
grassland	
evergreen forest	

N

E

S

W

39

North Africa

The hot Sahara Desert covers almost all of North Africa. Most of the desert is flat, but in some places the wind blows sand into big piles called dunes. Some sand dunes are as high as mountains. It hardly ever rains in the desert. That means there is very little water for people, plants, and animals. Most people live along the Mediterranean Sea. Here they can catch fish, and there is enough rain in the winter to grow fruits and vegetables.

▲ People in Niger build wells in the desert. The wells hold water for people and animals to drink.

Animals and plants

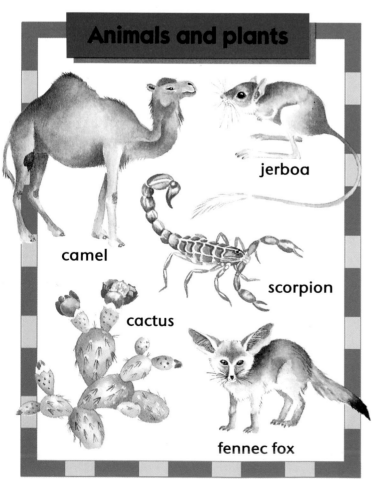

jerboa

camel

scorpion

cactus

fennec fox

Many tourists like to visit North Africa. They swim and relax on the beaches in Tunisia and Morocco or visit the pyramids in Egypt. These tall buildings are shaped like triangles. They were built thousands of years ago to be the burial tombs of Egyptian leaders.

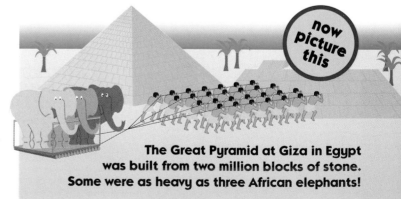

now picture this

The Great Pyramid at Giza in Egypt was built from two million blocks of stone. Some were as heavy as three African elephants!

Most people in North Africa live in towns of flat-roofed houses with thick walls to keep out the hot sun. But the Bedouin (BED-ou-win) live in the middle of the desert. They move from place to place to find **oases** – green, **fertile** areas in the desert. The Bedouin keep camels and goats. These animals can go for a long time without water.

▶ This worker in Fez, Morocco, soaks animal hides in special dyes. The dyes will make the leather waterproof.

▼ The Nile River is the longest river in the world. In Egypt it provides water to **irrigate** the farmland on its banks.

West Africa

The countries of West Africa run from Senegal in the north to Nigeria in the south. Some countries, such as Togo and Gambia, are tiny. Their **fertile** farms grow coffee, cocoa, and rubber trees. Other countries, like Nigeria, are large. Nigeria has more people than any other African country.

The capital city of Nigeria is Lagos (LAY-goss). It is also the industrial center. Nigeria is one of the world's biggest producers of oil. This has provided Nigerians with money to start modern, new industries such as clothing, food and steel production, and car manufacturing.

▲ These calabash bowls are made from gourds that grow on climbing vines.

Central Africa

Many countries form Central Africa. Zaire is the largest. The Zaire Basin is an enormous area of thick tropical rainforest on each side of the wide Zaire River. There are few roads. People travel by riverboats or in canoes. A crowded riverboat is a moving town. A market, drugstore, barber, and police are on board.

Oil is a big industry for some Central African countries, such as Cameroon and Gabon. Farming and lumber are also important. Farmers grow bananas, and a plant called cassava.

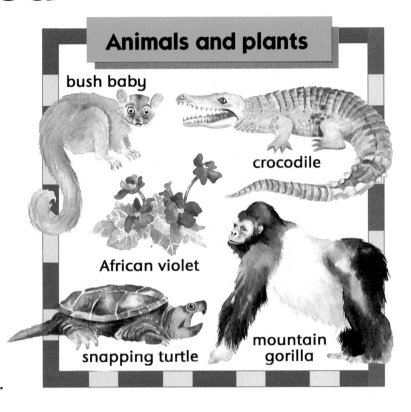

Animals and plants

bush baby

crocodile

African violet

snapping turtle

mountain gorilla

▼ This city in Zaire is built of mud huts. Its name is Mud Hut City.

East Africa

▼ East Africa has many lions. They live in groups called prides. Sometimes up to 30 lions live together.

The eight countries of East Africa are near the **Equator** where it is hot. But tall mountains and high grasslands help cool some areas. Much of East Africa is savannah, areas of grass and trees where many wild animals graze. Some places in the north, like Somalia and parts of Ethiopia, are very dry. Here, little rain falls to help grass, trees, or crops grow. This dry weather is called a drought. During a long drought, people and animals can find very little to eat.

Many groups of people live in East Africa. They include the Turkana, Masai (mah-SIGH), and Kikuyu (key-KOO-you). They are farmers, fishers, craftspeople, and workers in city industries. Whole families, including aunts and uncles, cousins, and grandparents often live together.

The Great Rift Valley divides East Africa. This **valley** was formed by **earthquakes** millions of years ago. It is nearly half a mile deep in some places.

Many tourists go to East Africa to visit its animal reserves. These are areas where wild animals are protected. The reserves are home to elephants, lions, leopards, giraffes, rhinoceroses, and other animals. It is against the law to hunt the animals. But **poachers** sometimes kill them for their skins, horns, or tusks.

▶ This Masai boy is practicing a dance. He is wearing a cloth colored with dye made from Kenya's clay soil.

Animals and plants

cheetah

acacia

pangolin

guinea fowl

zebra

flamingo

Southern Africa

Most of Southern Africa is warm and sunny all year. But in some high places, like the Cape Mountains in the country of South Africa, the winters can be cool and wet. The 11 countries of Southern Africa are south of the **Equator**. Two of the great African rivers, the Zambezi (zam-BEE-zee) and the Limpopo, flow through the east to the Indian Ocean. The Kalahari Desert is in the west, along the Atlantic Coast.

The countries of South Africa, Zimbabwe (zim-BOB-way), Angola, and Zambia are rich in diamonds, gold, iron, and copper. South Africa has more diamonds and gold than any other country. People from nearby countries, such as Botswana, come to work in the mines.

▲ Mine workers in Zambia drill for copper far below the ground.

Dutch people first settled in South Africa in 1651. Many more white Europeans arrived in the 1800s. For years, white South Africans controlled the country, even though there were many more black South Africans. Black South Africans were not allowed to vote, hold office, or even live among whites because of a law called apartheid (ah-PAR-tate). Now apartheid has ended. Blacks and whites will try to run their country together.

Animals and plants

aardvark

ostrich

baobab

welwitschsia

white rhino

lemur

▼ Cape Town lies at the tip of South Africa.

The San live in the Kalahari Desert. There is not enough rain to grow crops, but some fruits and flowers can grow here. The San hunt animals and gather fruit to eat.

now picture this

The San find water at tiny "sipwells" in the desert. They suck up water through hollow sticks and store it in ostrich eggshells.

▼ These people are grinding grain to make flour. They live on the **island** of Madagascar.

See also ANIMALS AND NATURE Farm, Forest, Mountain, Octopus, Weather

Europe

The continent of Europe is bordered by the Arctic and Atlantic Oceans in the north and west, and the Mediterranean Sea in the south. It is the only continent in the world without a desert. Mountains, forests, rivers, and fields surround its cities, towns, and villages. There are more than 40 countries in Europe. Each has its own languages, foods and history.

Arctic Circle

Lapland

FINLAND

Helsinki

Tallinn
ESTONIA

LATVIA
Riga

LITHUANIA
Vilnius

SWEDEN

Gulf of Bothnia

Baltic Sea

POLAND
Warsaw

Stockholm

NORWAY
Oslo

Copenhagen
DENMARK

Berlin

Prague
CZECH REPUBLIC

GERMANY

LUXEMBOURG

Rhine

NETHERLANDS
Amsterdam

Brussels
BELGIUM

Paris
Seine River

North Sea

UNITED KINGDOM

London

English Channel

IRELAND
Dublin

Reykjavik
ICELAND

ATLANTIC OCEAN

48

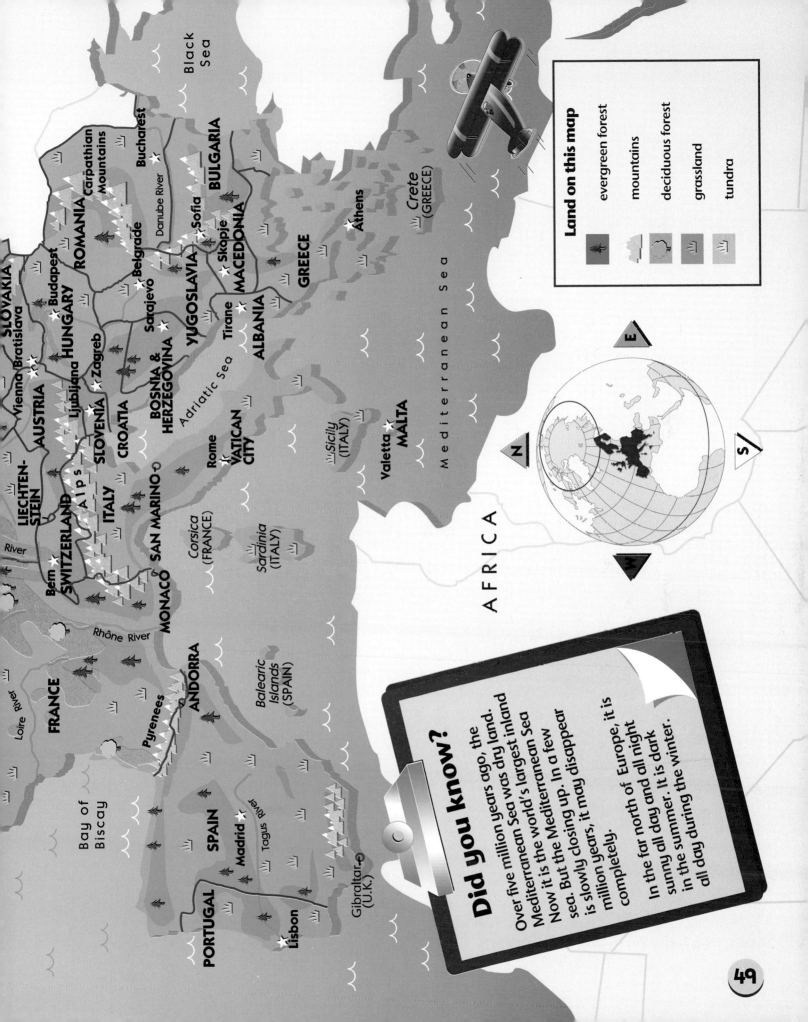

Black Sea

Carpathian Mountains

Bucharest ★

BULGARIA

ROMANIA

Danube River

Sofia ★

Belgrade ★

Skopje ★

MACEDONIA

YUGOSLAVIA

Sarajevo ★

Tirane ★

Athens ★

GREECE

ALBANIA

Crete (GREECE)

Mediterranean Sea

SLOVAKIA

Bratislava ★
Vienna ★

Budapest ★

HUNGARY

Ljubljana ★

Zagreb ★

AUSTRIA

BOSNIA & HERZEGOVINA

SLOVENIA

CROATIA

Adriatic Sea

LIECHTEN-STEIN

Bern ★

SWITZERLAND

Alps

ITALY

SAN MARINO ○

Rome ★

VATICAN CITY

Sicily (ITALY)

Valetta ★

MALTA

MONACO

Corsica (FRANCE)

Sardinia (ITALY)

Rhône River

River

Loire River

FRANCE

ANDORRA

Pyrenees

Bay of Biscay

Balearic Islands (SPAIN)

PORTUGAL

SPAIN

Madrid ★

Tagus River

Gibraltar ○ (U.K.)

Lisbon ★

AFRICA

N
W ◄
► E
S

Land on this map

evergreen forest

mountains

deciduous forest

grassland

tundra

Did you know?

Over five million years ago, the Mediterranean Sea was dry land. Now it is the world's largest inland sea. But the Mediterranean is slowly closing up. In a few million years, it may disappear completely.

In the far north of Europe, it is sunny all day and all night in the summer. It is dark all day during the winter.

Northern Europe

▼ Norway's coast has many long, narrow inlets of sea water. They are called fjords (fee-YORDS).

The countries of Norway, Sweden, Finland, Lithuania, Estonia, Latvia, Denmark, and Iceland make up Northern Europe. Here it is cool even in the summer and very cold in the winter. The north is bare and rocky. To the south, there are mountains, forests, and lakes. The south also has cities, towns, and villages where most Northern Europeans live.

The far north of Europe lies inside the Arctic Circle. This is a line that mapmakers draw around the top of the world. It divides the icy **region** around the North Pole from the warmer lands to the south. Parts of Europe near the Arctic Circle are too rocky and hilly for farming. Instead, people who live here catch fish to eat.

Animals and plants

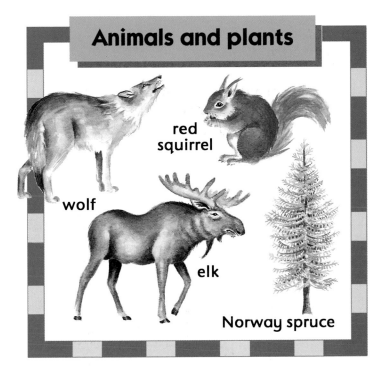

red squirrel

wolf

elk

Norway spruce

Northern Europe has forests full of spruce, larch, and pine trees. These trees are cut down and used to build homes. The wood is also used to make toys, furniture, paper, and matches.

▼ Legoland is a theme park in Denmark. Here, visitors can walk around miniature models of famous buildings made from plastic bricks.

Part of northern Finland and Sweden is called Lapland. The nomadic Sami live here. They keep reindeer for their milk, meat, and leather.

▶ The Sami often wear brightly colored outfits decorated with beads. Some Sami have sleighs to take tourists for rides across the frozen **tundra**.

Western Europe

Western Europe has many different kinds of land. The Alps, the highest mountains in Europe, are in the south. Some countries, like Belgium, are very low and flat. Others, like Britain and Ireland, are **islands**. The weather in most of this **region** is warm and wet. That is because a warm current of water called the Gulf Stream in the Atlantic Ocean is absorbed into the air over Western Europe.

▼ The Alps cover most of Switzerland. Here, many children can ski by the age of seven.

▼ In London, England, at the ceremony of "Trooping the Colour," the Queen inspects her troops. This ceremony has been taking place for hundreds of years.

Western Europe is a mix of countryside and cities. It is one of the most important industrial areas in the world. Factory workers here make cars, glass, chocolate, dishwashers, and other goods. In the countryside, farmers grow barley and other cereals and raise cows to make products like cheese and butter.

Busy streets

Tourists from all over the world visit Europe to see ancient buildings and ruins and cities like London, Rome, and Paris. Although the cities can be crowded, there is a lot of quiet countryside around, where wild plants and animals live.

▶ Shoppers and tourists fill the narrow streets of Amsterdam in the Netherlands.

Animals and plants

dragonfly

blackberry

poppy

oak

green woodpecker

fox

salmon

owl

hedgehog

The Mediterranean

▼ This village is on the **volcanic island** of Santorini, in Greece.

The countries of Spain, France, Italy, and Greece border the Mediterranean Sea. People have lived in these countries for thousands of years. Today, they can still see the ruins of buildings from these early **civilizations**. Some of the monuments and temples are more than 2,000 years old.

Millions of tourists come to the Mediterranean for its long, beautiful summers. They stay in towns and resorts along the coast. The hot sun and warm water are also good for farming and fishing. Markets sell fresh fruits and vegetables, such as peppers, tomatoes, and eggplants, and seafood, such as sardines and squid.

Many Mediterranean farmers grow olive trees. In the fall, they pick the olives and press them to make olive oil. Other farmers grow grapes, from which they make wine, and juicy fruits like oranges and melons.

▼ In Europe, merchants weigh goods in kilos and grams rather than pounds and ounces.

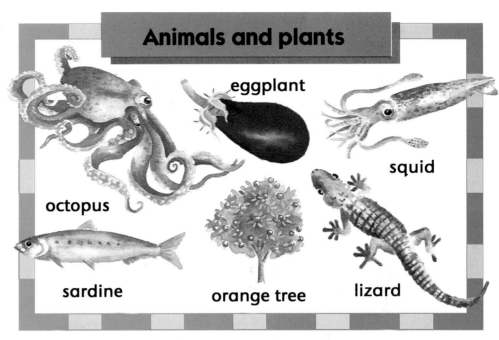

Animals and plants

octopus

eggplant

squid

sardine

orange tree

lizard

Eastern Europe

The countries of Eastern Europe are located between Western Europe and Russia. The weather is cold in the winter and warm in the summer. Much of Eastern Europe is covered with forest. The rest is farmland, cities, towns, and villages. Many people work on farms or in coal, iron, and copper mines. Others live and work in big industrial cities like Warsaw in Poland, and Prague in the Czech (CHECK) Republic.

▶ Some wooden Romanian houses have patterns carved into them.

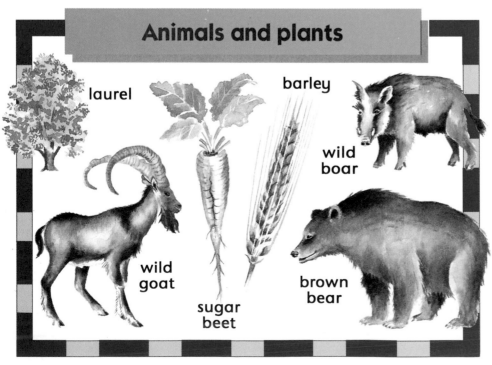

Animals and plants

laurel

barley

wild boar

wild goat

sugar beet

brown bear

Many Eastern European countries, like Poland and Hungary, have flat, **fertile plains.** These plains are perfect for farming. Farmers here grow wheat, barley, potatoes, and oats, and raise cattle and hogs for meat. These crops and meats are ingredients in many favorite Eastern European foods, like sausages, smoked meat, spicy stews, and dumplings.

Eastern Europeans have many festivals that have been celebrated for centuries. At the festivals, people dance and listen to folk songs. These songs tell stories about the land and the people. Children learn the songs from their parents.

▼ **Polish children wear traditional embroidered outfits to celebrate their Harvest Festival. This festival is held in the fall, when the crops have been gathered.**

**Time for a change
Communist** governments ruled Eastern European countries for more than 40 years. These governments did not let people choose their own leaders. But now people are setting up other kinds of government.

Russia and Its Neighbors

Russia is the largest country in the world. It is so big that it has 11 time zones. That means when it is breakfast time in the west, it is late afternoon in the east. Russia and the smaller countries around it have vast forests, mountains, farmland, **plains**, and deserts. The western part of this **region** is on the continent of Europe. The eastern part is in Asia. The high Ural mountains divide the two parts.

St. Petersburg

Minsk

BELARUS

MOLDOVA

Chisinau

Kiev

Moscow

UKRAINE

EUROPEAN RUSSIA

Black Sea

Caucasus Mountains

Ural Mountains

Volga River

s t e p p e

Ob River

GEORGIA

Yerevan

T'bilisi

Irtysh River

ARMENIA

AZERBAIJAN

Baku

Caspian Sea

Aral Sea

KAZAKHSTAN

N

TURKMENISTAN

Kara Kum Desert

Ashgabat

Lake Balkash

W

E

UZBEKISTAN

Tashkent

Bishkek

Almaty

Dushanbe

KYRGYZSTAN

S

TAJIKISTAN

58

Land on this map

 evergreen forest

 grassland

 mountains

 desert

 tundra

 deciduous forest

ARCTIC
OCEAN

Arctic Circle

Did you know?

Oymyakon is the coldest town in the world. The **temperature** often drops to -50° **Fahrenheit.**

Lake Baikal is the deepest lake in the world. If 950 people stood on each other's shoulders, the water would still cover them.

It takes seven days to travel on the Trans-Siberian Railway from Moscow in western Russia to Vladivostok in the east.

S i b e r i a

Oymyakon●

ASIAN RUSSIA

NORTH
PACIFIC
OCEAN

Yenisei River

Lena River

t a i g a

Lake
Baikal

Trans-Siberian Railway

●Vladivostok

West of the Urals

The Ural Mountains divide Russia into two parts. Most Russians live in the western part. Here there are big cities like Moscow and St. Petersburg. The west also has the best farmland. Farmers grow fields of wheat and raise cattle. Russia's neighbors to the south, like Georgia, Ukraine, and Azerbaijan (AH-zer-by-jan), are also farming countries. The east is rugged and extends north into the Arctic Circle.

Russia has many industries, including shipbuilding, steel making, and coal mining. Many of the factories where clothes and other products are made are old and cannot make all the things people want to buy.

▲ In Moscow, the capital of Russia, dancers perform traditional folk dances.

Some of the world's greatest music and ballet dancers have come from Russia. The Kirov, Moscow City, and Bolshoi (BOWL-shoy) ballet companies perform all over the world.

Animals and plants

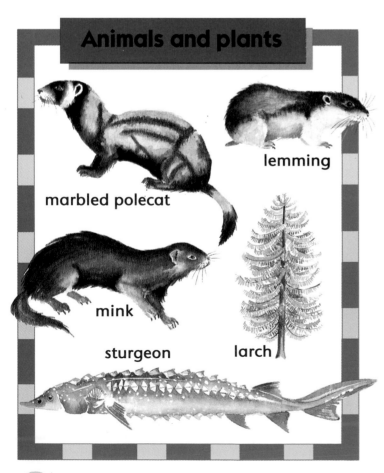

marbled polecat

lemming

mink

larch

sturgeon

Russia and its neighbors used to be all one nation. It was ruled by a form of government called **Communism.** The government ran the farms and factories. People were poor, and goods were expensive. In 1991, the communist government ended.

Now each country is independent. Many things are changing. People are allowed to travel more freely. Some people have started new businesses. Others are running for office.

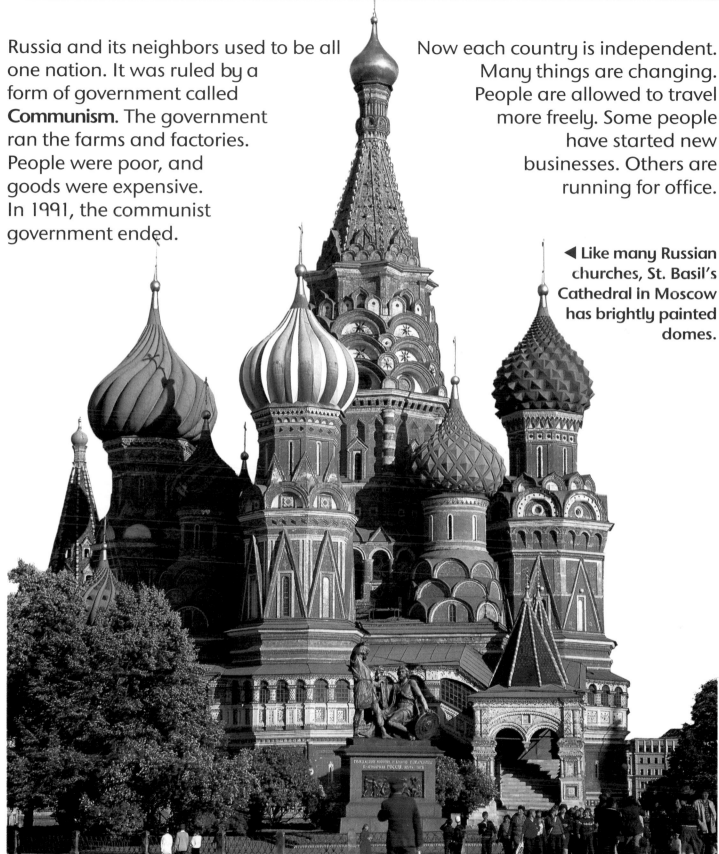

◀ Like many Russian churches, St. Basil's Cathedral in Moscow has brightly painted domes.

East of the Urals

East of the Ural Mountains is a huge area of Russia called Siberia. It is one of the coldest places on earth. Few people live there. The northern part of Siberia is icy wilderness called **tundra**. To the south is a huge forest of pine and fir trees called taiga (TIE-gah). The taiga is the largest forest in the world. It is home to many bears and wolves.

Rich mineral resources lie underground in Siberia. Here workers mine diamonds, gold, silver, and copper. In nearby Uzbekistan (Uz-BEK-i-stan), they drill for oil and mine coal.

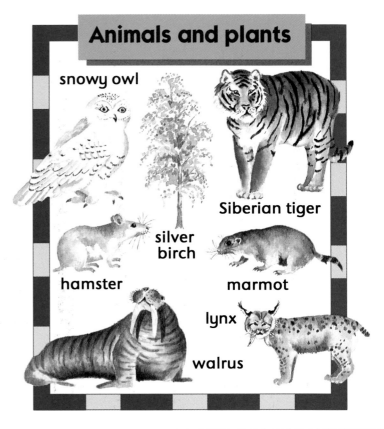

Animals and plants

snowy owl

silver birch

Siberian tiger

hamster

marmot

lynx

walrus

▼ Parts of Siberia are so cold that the ground is frozen. That makes mining very difficult.

▼ **Nomads** in Siberia follow their herds of reindeer from place to place as the animals search for food.

In other countries south of Siberia, farmers produce cotton, rice, and silk. In the country of Turkmenistan, people are able to grow fruit in the Kara Kum Desert in **fertile** areas called **oases**.

The steppe is a dry, grassy **plain** southwest of Siberia. There are no trees here. On the steppe, the sun is hot, but the winds are cold. Wild hamsters and marmots take shelter in their underground burrows.

▶ This Siberian farmer raises chickens for eggs and meat. The nearest city is hundreds of miles away.

Southwest and Southern

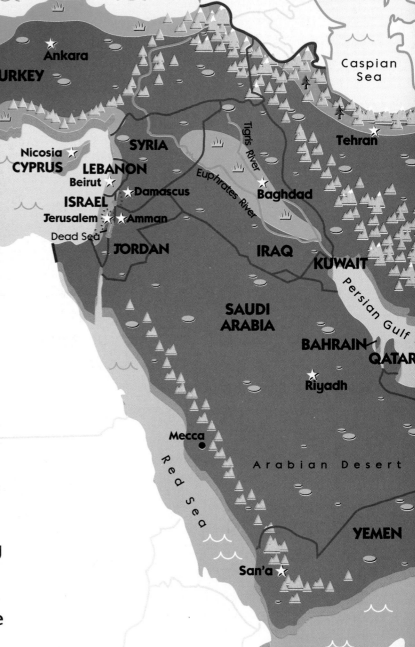

Did you know?

Mount Everest in the Himalayas is the world's highest mountain above sea level. It is more than 5 miles high.

The brightly colored turbans some men wear in northern India are 40 feet long when they are unwrapped.

Asian elephants live to be up to 80 years old.

TURKEY
Ankara

Caspian Sea

Nicosia
CYPRUS
SYRIA
Tigris River
Tehran

LEBANON
Beirut
Damascus
Euphrates River
Baghdad

ISRAEL
Jerusalem
Amman
Dead Sea
JORDAN
IRAQ
KUWAIT

SAUDI ARABIA
Persian Gulf

BAHRAIN
QATAR

Riyadh

Mecca
Arabian Desert

Red Sea

YEMEN

San'a

AFRICA

Southwest and Southern Asia are bordered by the Mediterranean and Red Seas in the west. In the east, they are cut off from China by the high Himalayan Mountains. Much of Southwest Asia is hot and dry. People live in cities on the edges of its many large, dry deserts. Southern Asia has many crowded countries. India is the biggest. Its millions of people live in large cities or in thousands of villages in the countryside.

64

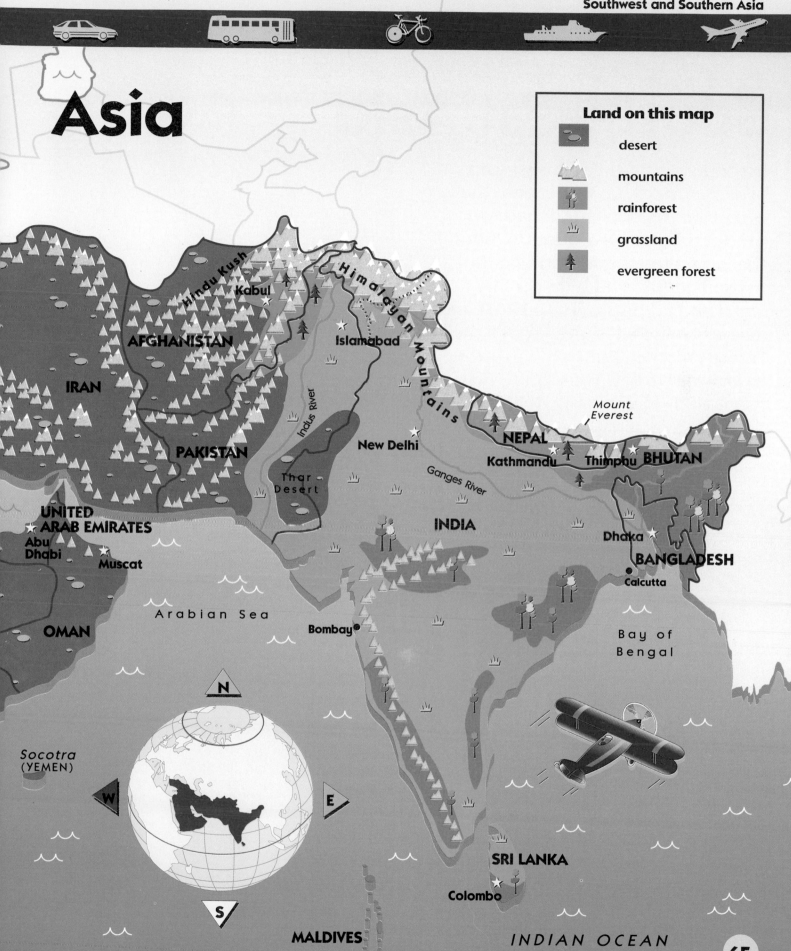

Asia

Land on this map

desert

mountains

rainforest

grassland

evergreen forest

Hindu Kush

Kabul

Himalayan Mountains

AFGHANISTAN

Islamabad

IRAN

Indus River

PAKISTAN

New Delhi

Thar Desert

Mount Everest

NEPAL

Kathmandu

Thimphu BHUTAN

Ganges River

UNITED ARAB EMIRATES

Abu Dhabi

Muscat

INDIA

Dhaka

BANGLADESH

Calcutta

OMAN

Arabian Sea

Bombay

Bay of Bengal

N

Socotra (YEMEN)

W

E

S

SRI LANKA

Colombo

MALDIVES

INDIAN OCEAN

Southwest Asia

In many places in Southwest Asia, oil and natural gas lie beneath the desert sand. People drill these products from the ground. Most of the land is too dry for farming. But the soil on the land between the Tigris and Euphrates (you-FRATE-eez) Rivers is so rich it is often called the Fertile Crescent. Farmers here grow cotton and dates. The world's first farms and cities were built here thousands of years ago.

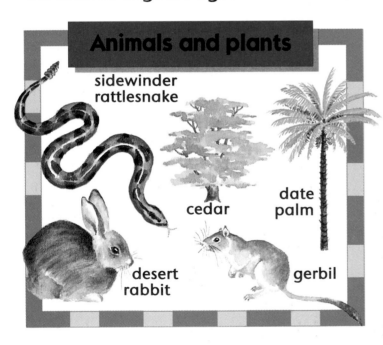

Animals and plants

sidewinder rattlesnake

cedar

date palm

desert rabbit

gerbil

Countries near the Persian Gulf sell oil to people around the world. The oil is used to make soap, nylon, and gas. Every day, millions of gallons of gas are burned in cars around the world.

▲ The country of Kuwait was once poor. But oil was found here in 1938. Now Kuwait is very wealthy.

now picture this

The Dead Sea in Israel is so salty that you cannot sink!

Three of the world's great religions began in Southwest Asia. The religion of the Jews is called Judaism and was started by Abraham 4,000 years ago. Christianity, based on the teachings of Jesus, began 2,000 years ago. Muhammad founded the religion of Islam about 600 years later. Today, these religions have followers all over the world.

▶ The Kuchi are **nomads** who live in the high, bare mountains of Afghanistan.

▼ Muslims follow the religion of Islam. They pray facing Mecca, their most holy city, which is in western Saudi Arabia.

Southern Asia

India, Pakistan, Bhutan, Bangladesh, Sri Lanka (shri-LAN-ka), and Nepal are in Southern Asia. Most of the people live in small villages. Many build their homes of mud and straw and farm rice, peppers, peanuts, and tea. Most of the farms are small and people grow only enough for their own needs. Southern Asia also has big cities, such as Bombay and Calcutta.

▼ Some Indian farmers cannot afford modern machinery to help them.

It is almost always hot and dry in Southern Asia. But every summer the monsoon comes. This is a hot wind that comes from the Indian Ocean, bringing a lot of heavy rain. It can cause problems because rivers overflow and **flood** village streets and farms. But many people welcome the monsoon because the rain helps their crops grow.

◀ An Indian king built the Taj Mahal in the 1600s to show his love for his wife.

▶ Thousands of Hindu people come to bathe in the Ganges River in India. The river waters are holy in the Hindu religion.

Village life is hard. Most farmers live in mud huts with just one or two rooms. The family sleeps on cots woven from string. They have to get their water from nearby wells. Women often carry the water home in clay pots which they balance on their heads.

Hikers like to climb in the Himalayan Mountains. They are the highest mountains in the world. Some parts are still being formed.

Animals and plants

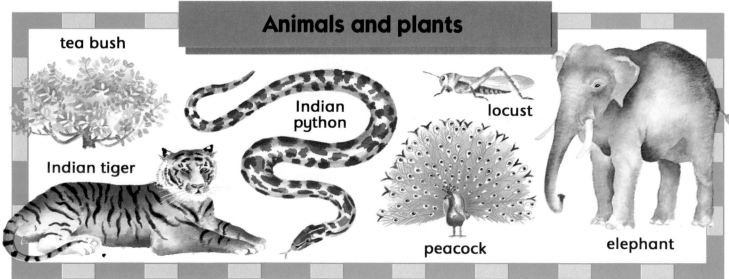

tea bush

Indian tiger

Indian python

locust

peacock

elephant

China, Japan,

China is the third largest country in the world. About one out of five of all the world's people live here. Most Chinese live along rivers in the east, where the **climate** is warm and wet. The rest of the country is mostly mountains and desert. China has one of the oldest **civilizations** in the world.

Did you know?

Long ago, people in China built a huge wall to keep their enemies out. It is called the Great Wall. The wall is so big that it can be seen from the moon!

Japan has the world's fastest passenger train. It travels between the cities of Tokyo and Osaka. It is so fast the Japanese call it "the bullet train."

Ulan Bator ★

MONGOLIA

Gobi Desert

Taklimakan Desert

Great Wall of China

Himalayan Mountains

T i b e t

Mount Everest

N

W

E

S

Land on this map

 grassland

 mountains

 rainforest

 desert

 evergreen forest

 tundra

and North and South Korea

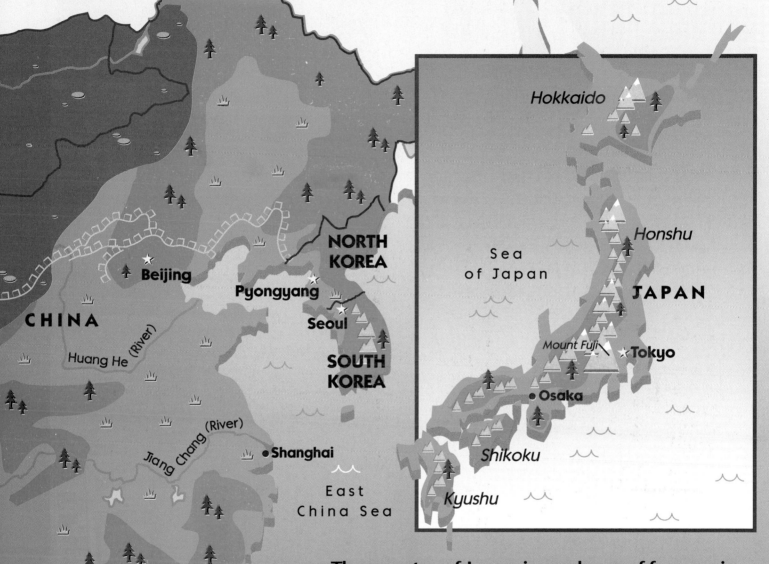

NORTH
KOREA

Beijing

Pyongyang

CHINA

Seoul

Huang He (River)

SOUTH
KOREA

Jiang Chang (River)

Shanghai

East
China Sea

Hokkaido

Honshu

Sea
of Japan

JAPAN

Mount Fuji

Tokyo

Osaka

Shikoku

Kyushu

T'aipei

Macao

Hong
Kong

TAIWAN

South
China Sea

The country of Japan is made up of four main **islands** and 4,000 small ones. These islands lie between the Sea of Japan and the Pacific Ocean. Japanese call their country Nippon, or "source of the sun," because the climate here is so sunny and warm. To the west are North and South Korea. These countries are on the Asian mainland. Most Koreans live on the coast or near rivers.

71

China, Hong Kong, and Taiwan

China has more people than any other country in the world. More than one **billion** people live here. Most Chinese grow rice in fields called paddies. The farmers **flood** the paddies with water to help the rice grow. China grows more rice than any other country. Other Chinese live in big cities like Shanghai (SHANG-high) and Beijing (bay-JING). Most of them do not have cars. Instead they walk or ride bicycles to work.

Animals and plants

golden pheasant

yak

giant panda

bamboo

Bactrian camel

▲ This woman is selling noodles. Noodles and rice are China's main foods.

Because there are so many people, China has always had a hard time feeding everyone. In 1948, a **Communist** government took over the farms, factories, and mines. It says it can feed more people that way. It makes rules about how much money people can make and how much they will pay for food and other things. But most people are still poor. Today, some Chinese are allowed to own small businesses and farms.

Hong Kong is made up of a small piece of the Asian mainland and more than 200 **islands**. It is a beautiful and important **port** on the southern coast of China. Hong Kong is full of banks, business offices, and shops. Factories here make clothes and toys that are sold all over the world.

Hong Kong is one of the most crowded places on earth. It is jammed with skyscrapers. Many people must live on houseboats.

▶ **Houseboats tied together in Hong Kong harbor.**

◀ **Rice drying near a farm in Taiwan.**

Taiwan is a mountainous island in the South China Sea. People here grow rice, tea, sugar cane, and pineapples. Factories make toys, car parts, electronics, and other products that are sold around the world. Many people came here from China when Communists took over.

73

Japan and North and South Korea

Most Japanese live in modern cities, like Tokyo, on the coasts. Japan's cities are important manufacturing centers. Japanese-made cars, computers, computer games, and televisions are sold all over the world. These products help make Japan a wealthy country.

▶ Japan's capital, Tokyo, is one of the largest cities in the world.

▲ Mount Fuji (FOO-gee) on Honshu Island last **erupted** nearly 300 years ago.

Japan's hot summers and mild winters are good for farming. Farmers dig wide, flat steps into the hillsides to make space for their crops. They grow rice, potatoes, and fruit. But since there isn't much land for farming, most of Japan's food comes from the sea. People here eat fish almost every day, along with lots of rice and noodles.

▼ These girls are playing drums during a Japanese festival.

Animals and plants

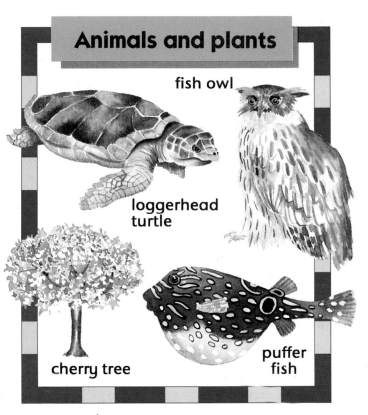

fish owl

loggerhead turtle

cherry tree

puffer fish

The Japanese are used to feeling the earth shake and shudder. Japan has hundreds of **earthquakes** each year. Sometimes an earthquake happens under the sea. It makes a big wave called a tsunami (sue-NOM-ee), which can damage buildings on the coast. Japan also has many wind storms called typhoons (tie-FOONS).

Korea was divided into two countries, North and South Korea, by a war that ended in 1953. The two countries are surrounded by water on three sides, and North Korea is connected to China.

▲ Buildings like this one in North Korea are called pagodas. Each story has its own roof.

Southeast Asia

MYANMAR

Hanoi

LAOS

Vientiane

Irrawaddy River

Mekong River

THAILAND

VIETNAM

South
China Sea

CAMBODIA

Yangon

Bangkok

Phnom
Penh

*INDIAN
OCEAN*

Manila

PHILIP

BRUNEI

Kuala Lumpur

M A L A Y S I A

SINGAPORE

Borneo

Sumatra

I N D O

Java

Jakarta

Bogor

Southeast Asia
has ten countries.
Some, such as
Thailand (TIE-land)
and Vietnam, are on
the Asian mainland.
Other countries, such as
Indonesia, are made up of
volcanic islands off the coast.
Southeast Asia is close to the
Equator, so the weather here is very
hot and sunny. Rainforests, **volcanoes**,
and mountains cover most of the land.

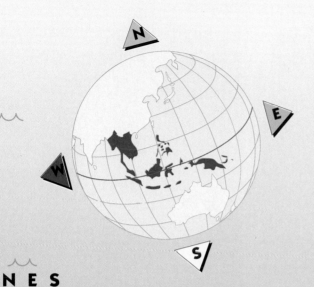

N

E

W

S

Did you know?

In Bogor on the **island** of Java, there is thunder almost every night of the year.

The rafflesia plant in Malaysia has the largest flower in the world. It is wider than an adult's arm and can weigh as much as a watermelon!

The country of Indonesia is made up of more than thirteen thousand small islands.

Equato

P I N E S

PACIFIC OCEAN

Celebes

N E S I A

PAPUA NEW GUINEA

New Guinea

 Port Moresby

AUSTRALIA

Land on this map

	rainforest
	mountains

Southeast Asia

Much of the land of Southeast Asia is covered with thick rainforest, and there are few roads. People travel by boat on rivers. They build their villages on the riverbanks. They build their homes high on stilts to keep them dry when the rivers **flood**.

The rainforest is noisy with the calls of orang-utans, monkeys, frogs, birds, and insects. Sometimes these animals lose their homes when farmers cut down trees to grow new crops.

▲ This house in the Philippines is made of a hard-stemmed plant called bamboo.

Animals and plants

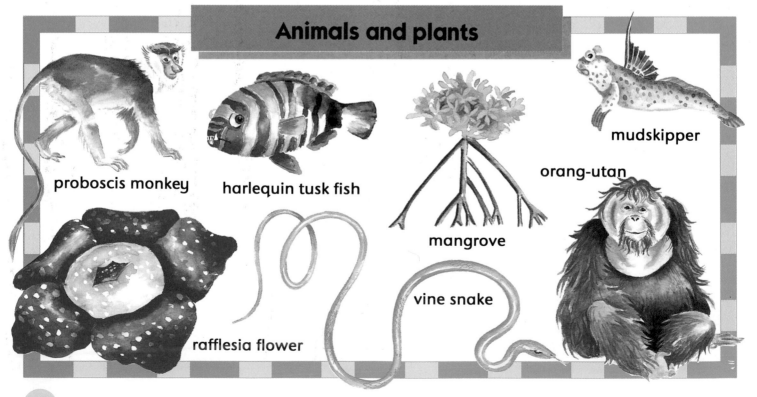

proboscis monkey

harlequin tusk fish

mangrove

mudskipper

orang-utan

rafflesia flower

vine snake

In Cambodia, Vietnam, and other countries, many people grow rice. Rubber, spices, and coffee are also important crops.

▶ In Java, Indonesia, women and children get rubber from rubber trees. They cut deep grooves in the bark and the rubber trickles down into cups.

▼ In Bangkok, Thailand (TIE-land), there is a floating market. Farmers come to the city by boat to sell their goods.

Australia and New Zealand

Australia is the smallest continent in the world. It is south of the **Equator** and is surrounded by the Indian Ocean on the west and the Pacific Ocean on the east. It is on the opposite side of the world from Europe and North America. This means that the time of day is also opposite. When it is daytime in Australia and New Zealand, it is nighttime on the other side of the world.

Did you know?

New Zealand has more **volcanoes** than any other country. Auckland, its biggest city, is built on top of 60 dead volcanoes!

The Maori of New Zealand rub noses with their guests to welcome them.

Because Australia is in the Southern Hemisphere, Christmas comes during summer vacation.

INDIAN OCEAN

Darwin

Northern Territory

A U S T R A L I A

Alice Springs

Uluru (Ayers Rock)

Gibson Desert

Great Victoria Desert

South Australia

Lake Eyre

Western Australia

Perth

Adelaide

N
W
E
S

SOLOMON ISLANDS

PACIFIC OCEAN

Land on this map

grassland

mountains

desert

VANUATU

Coral Sea

WESTERN SAMOA

FIJI

New Caledonia (FRANCE)

TONGA

Queensland

Great Barrier Reef

Great Dividing Range

Darling River

New South Wales

Wagga Wagga

Murray River

Victoria

Australian Capital Territory

• Brisbane

• Sydney

• Canberra

• Melbourne

Tasmania

• Hobart

New Zealand is a small country in the Pacific Ocean, east of Australia. It is made up of several **islands**. The biggest are North Island and South Island. They have volcanoes, farmland, mountains, and forests. On this map, New Zealand is shown larger and closer to Australia than it should be so you can see more.

Auckland

Rotorua

North Island

Mount Taranaki

Wellington

Southern Alps

Christchurch

South Island

NEW ZEALAND

Stewart Island

Australia

▼ The giant Uluru rock has many dark caves.

Australia is the sixth largest country in the world. Most of the country is desert and bush-covered land called the outback. Here, there are few towns. Most people live in the south, where the **climate** is cooler and the land is good for farming. The big southern cities are Sydney, Brisbane, Melbourne, and Adelaide.

▲ These girls are college students in Alice Springs.

Most Australians are **descendants** of Europeans. Native Australians are called Aborigines (ah-buh-RIJ-in-ees). These people have lived in Australia for fifty thousand years. Today, some Aborigines still live in the outback, but many live and work in towns and cities.

Australia is one of the world's biggest producers of wool and beef. Farmers raise sheep and cows on cattle stations in the outback. Many children who live here are far from schools. They talk to their teachers by two-way radio and send in their homework by mail.

The Great Barrier Reef lies off Australia's northeast coast. It is made of coral, which is the hard skeletons of tiny sea creatures called polyps (POL-ips). Many of the polyps still live in the coral.

▼ Bright tropical fish swim near the Great Barrier Reef.

Animals and plants

cockatoo

estuarine crocodile

gum tree

koala

dingo

kookaburra

platypus

emu

red kangaroo

Some unusual animals, such as the koala and platypus, live only in Australia. The most common of these animals is the big, gray kangaroo. It can be found all over the country, especially in parks and on farmland.

New Zealand

The Maori (MAUW-ree) were the first people to live in New Zealand. They arrived more than 1,000 years ago. They came in canoes from other **islands** in the Pacific Ocean. People from Europe started to come to New Zealand about 200 years ago. Today, most New Zealanders are **descendants** of those Europeans.

▶ This farmhouse is at the bottom of Mount Taranaki, one of North Island's many **volcanoes**.

▼ Children in New Zealand play old Maori games.

Many New Zealanders live and work on farms. They raise sheep for meat and wool. Other farmers grow fruits and grains. But most New Zealanders live in towns and cities like the capital, Wellington. The largest city is Auckland. Here, clothes and lumber are manufactured and sold.

Animals and plants

tuatara

weta

pohutukawa

punga

takahe

kiwi

kakapo

New Zealand is home to several unusual wild animals and plants that are found only on its islands. The kiwi, the punga, the kakapo, and the tuatara are a few examples.

▲ A **geyser** is a jet of hot water that escapes from underground like steam from a teapot. This geyser is near Rotorua, North Island.

Antarctica

The continent of Antarctica is located at the bottom of the world. The South Pole is at its center. Antarctica is the coldest and windiest place on earth. It is covered with ice up to 3 miles thick. Very few plants and animals can survive here, but penguins, fish, and seals live on the coast and in the seas. No people live on Antarctica permanently, but scientists and tourists visit.

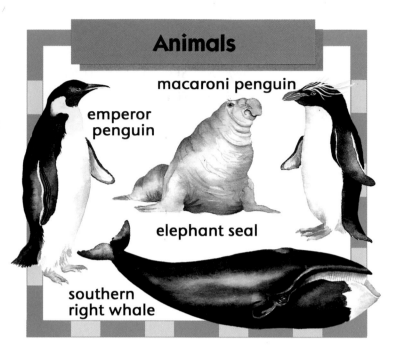

Animals

macaroni penguin

emperor penguin

elephant seal

southern right whale

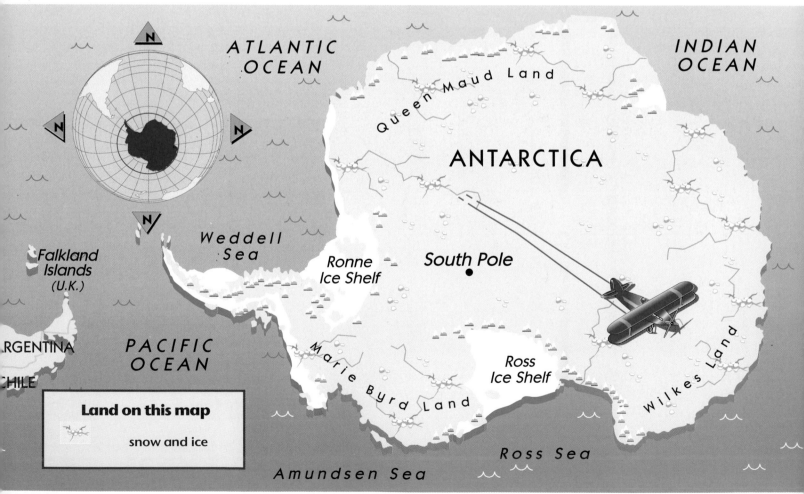

N

ATLANTIC OCEAN

INDIAN OCEAN

Queen Maud Land

ANTARCTICA

Weddell Sea

Falkland Islands (U.K.)

Ronne Ice Shelf

South Pole

ARGENTINA

PACIFIC OCEAN

Marie Byrd Land

Ross Ice Shelf

Wilkes Land

CHILE

Land on this map

snow and ice

Ross Sea

Amundsen Sea

86

There are no countries in Antarctica, but several nations have built scientific **research stations** here. Scientists come to study the **climate** and the ice. Some countries also want to explore Antarctica for gold and other minerals. But other countries want to make Antarctica a world park.

Glossary

Ancestors The members of your family who lived and died many years ago.

Antarctic Circle A line drawn by mapmakers near the South Pole, at the bottom of the earth. Countries that lie near the Antarctic Circle are cold because the sun never rises high in the sky.

Arctic Circle A line drawn by mapmakers near the North Pole, at the top of the earth. Countries that lie near the Arctic Circle are cold because the sun never rises high in the sky.

Billion There are 1,000 millions in a billion.

Canyon Narrow, rocky land between steep cliffs.

Caribou A large North American deer.

Civilization A well-organized country or large group of people. Most modern civilizations have big cities, schools, hospitals, and museums.

Climate The sort of weather that is usual in a particular area or country.

Communism A set of ideas about the way a country should be run. The main idea is that all people should share all their money equally. In most communist countries, the government controls schools, farms, hospitals, and factories.

Descendants Your children and your children's children. You are descended from your parents and grandparents.

Earthquake When a piece of the earth's crust grinds against another piece, the ground trembles and the surface of the earth cracks open.

Eruption The explosion of hot gas and rock that spills out of a **volcano**.

Equator An imaginary line drawn by mapmakers around the middle of the earth. Countries that lie near the Equator are hot because that part of the world is closest to the sun.

Fahrenheit A measurement for telling how hot or cold something is.

Fertile Land that has soil which is good for growing healthy crops.

Flood A large amount of water covering an area that is usually dry. It is normally caused by very heavy rains.

Geyser Jets of hot water that escape from hot underground rock.

Globe An object shaped like a ball with a map of the earth on it.

Irrigate To supply dry farmland with water.

Island A piece of land that is surrounded by water on all sides.

Nomad A person who does not live in a fixed place. Nomadic people often take their animals, such as cattle, with them as they move around looking for food.

Oasis (oases) A place in the desert where water bubbles up to the surface from underground streams.

Peninsula An area of land that is almost an **island**. It is still attached to the mainland but is surrounded by water on three sides.

Plain A large, flat area of land with very few trees. In some countries, plains are also called prairies, steppes, or pampas.

Poacher A person who hunts animals that are living on protected or private land.

Port A town or area on the coast that has a harbor where ships can sail in and out to dock and deliver and collect goods.

Province A part, or area, of a country.

Region A particular area of land, such as the Arctic region around the North Pole, that has at least one common characteristic, such as climate, language, or landform.

Research station A place where scientists can study the animals, plants, minerals, landscape, weather, or people in an area.

Sandstone A type of rock made from sand. It is often used to make bricks for buildings.

State A particular area of some large countries whose boundaries are recognized and which has some form of government.

Symbol A code that stands for a real object. The symbol may be a shape or a small picture. For example, a picture of a tree is a symbol for a real forest on the maps in this encyclopedia.

Temperature How hot or cold something is.

Territory An area of land that is separate from but belongs to a country.

Tundra Land that has no trees and is frozen all the year round. Tundra is found mainly around the Arctic Circle and on very high mountains.

Valley A stretch of land that lies in between hills, often with a river flowing through it.

Volcanic island An **island** that is formed by the eruption of **volcanoes** beneath the ocean. Liquid rock emptying from the volcano forms layers which eventually rise above the ocean surface.

Volcano An opening in the earth's surface. where gases and very hot liquid rock escape. Volcanoes are found in mountain chains on land and under the sea.

Index

Madagascar *39, 47*
Madrid 49
Maine 21
Malabo 39
Malawi 39
Malaysia 76, 77
Maldive Islands 65
Mali 38
Malta 49
Managua 28
Manila 76
Manitoba 15
mantle of the earth 8
Maori *80, 84*
Maputo 39
Marie Byrd Land 86
Maryland 21
Masai *44, 45*
Massachusetts 21
Mauritania 38
Maya *30*
Mecca *64, 67*
Mediterranean Sea *38, 40, 48, 49, 64*
Mekong River 76
Melbourne *81, 82*
Mexico 20, *21*, 27, 28
Mexico City 20, *21*
Miami *21, 26*
Michigan 21
Minnesota 21
Minsk 58
Mississippi 21
Mississippi River *21, 24*
Missouri 21
Missouri River 21
Mogadishu 39
Moldova 58
Monaco 49
Mongolia 70
monsoon 68
Montana 21
Montevideo 29
Montreal *15, 19*
Monument Valley *20, 25*
Morocco *38, 40*
Moscow *58, 60, 61*
Mount Everest *64, 65, 70*
Mount Fuji *71, 74*
Mount Kilimanjaro 39
Mount Popocatépetl 21
Mount Rushmore *21, 24*

Mount Taranaki 81, 84
Mount Washington 21
mountain 12, 13, 18, 20, 23, 24, 25, 27, 34, 35, 46, 48, 50, 52, 58, 60, 62, 64, 67, 70, 73, 74, 76, 84
Mozambique 39
Murray River 81
Muscat 65
Myanmar 76

N

N'Djamena 39
Nairobi 39
Namibia 39
Native Americans *20, 27*
Nebraska 21
Nelson River 15
Nepal *65, 68*
Netherlands *48, 53*
Nevada 20
New Brunswick 15
New Caledonia 81
New Delhi 65
New Guinea 77
New Hampshire 21
New Jersey 21
New Mexico *21, 25*
New Orleans 21
New South Wales 81
New York 21
New York City *21*, 23
New Zealand 80, *81*, 84–85
Newfoundland 15
Niagara Falls 14, *15*, 21
Niamey 39
Nicaragua *28, 30*
Nicosia 64
Niger *38, 40*
Niger River 38
Nigeria *39, 42*
Nile River *38, 41*
nomad *63, 67*
North America 9, 10, 14–15, 16, 18, 19, 20–21, 22, 23, 24, 25, 26
North Atlantic Ocean 15
North Carolina 21
North Dakota 21
North Island 81
North Korea *71, 75*

North Pacific Ocean 59
North Pole 14, 50
North Sea 48
Northern Territory 80
Northwest Territories 15
Norway 14, 48, 50
Nouakchott 38
Nova Scotia 15

O

oasis 41, 63
Ob River 58
ocean 8, 10, 11, 12, 14, 15, 17, 19, 20, 21, 22, 24, 26, 28, 29, 32, 39, 46, 48, 49, 52, 59, 65, 68, 71, 76, 77, 80, 81, 84
Ohio 21
Ohio River 21
Oklahoma 21
Oman 65
Ontario 15
Orange River 39
Oregon 20
Orinoco River 28
Osaka 71
Oslo 48
Ottawa 15
Ouagadougou 39
Oymyakon 59

P

Pacific Ocean *10, 11*, 20, 24, *28–29, 71, 77, 80, 81, 86*
Pakistan *65*, 68
pampas *29*, 36
Panama *28*, 30
Panama Canal 28
Panama City 28
Pangaea 9
Papua New Guinea 77
Paraguay *29*, 36
Paramaribo 28
Paraná River 29
Paris 48, 53
Patagonia *29*, 37
Pennsylvania 21
Persian Gulf *64*, 66
Perth 80
Peru 28, *34, 35*
Philadelphia 21
Philippines *76, 78*

Phnom Penh 76
plain 18, 20, 24, 36, 56, 58, 63
plate of the earth 8
Poland *48, 56, 57*
Port Moresby 77
Portugal *49*
Prague 48
prairie 24
Pretoria 39
Prince Edward Island 15
Puerto Rico 28
Pyongyang 71
Pyrenees Mountains 49

Q

Qatar 64
Quebec 15
Quecha 34
Queen Elizabeth Islands 14
Queen Maud Land 86
Queensland 81
Quito 28

R

Rabat 38
rainforest 13, 29, 30, 32, 38, 43, 76, 78
Red Sea *38, 64*
Reykjavik 48
Rhine River 48–49
Rhode Island 21
Rhône River 49
Riga 48
Rio de Janeiro *29*, 32, 33
Rio Grande 20, *21*
Riyadh 64
Rocky Mountains *15*, 18, 20, 24, 25
Romania *49, 56*
Rome 49, 53
Ronne Ice Shelf 86
Ross Ice Shelf 86
Ross Sea 86
Rotorua *81, 85*
Russia *14, 48, 56, 58–59, 60–63*
Rwanda 39

S

Sahara Desert *38, 40*
Sami 51

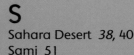